THE NEW BOOK OF FOLIAGE ARRANGEMENTS

THE NEW BOOK OF

FOLIAGE

ARRANGEMENTS

BY EMMA HODKINSON CYPHERS

77842

Hearthside Press Incorporated · Publishers · New York

CONTENTS

THE NEW BOOK OF FOLIAGE ARRANGEMENTS

1

THE APPEAL OF LEAVES

What would be the world without leaves? Their coloring matter (chlorophyll) is the only substance that can make the starch or sugar essential to all life, including that of man. And so leaves mean existence. The artist's task is to see and feel the charm of their patterned shapes. Artists of all time, working in all media, have used the leaves of plants as a source of inspiration second only to the human form.

HERITAGE OF THE CENTURIES

Murals displaying leaves of the original Tree of Life, the date palm, cut into rounded symmetry much as is done by many flower arrangers today have been found on the walls of ancient Egyptian tombs. And we can look on century-old architecture ornamented with sculptured foliage. Immortalized on the Corinthian pillar of ancient Greece, the favored acan-

thus leaf still furnishes a handsome and popular pattern on buttresses and pillars of support, with the bay-tree (laurel) a close second.

A rich harvest of legends and myths gives evidence of ancient man's reverent regard for leaves. Long before the Christian era, a three-leaf plant was held in high esteem, as representative of the three divisions of Nature—the earth, the sea, and the sky. Some leaves they endowed with grand and noble character. Among the most interesting is the box. Long before it was popular in English gardens, primitive man considered it the emblem of constancy and endurance. Some were dedicated to pagan deities. The vigor of the oak, for instance, was power and strength personified in Jupiter and Zeus. Foliage was woven into swags and garlands carried in religious processions, and fashioned into crowns worn to the altars. In fact, a leaf crown was the highest

1

honor man could bestow. Ceremonial vessels were decorated with leaf patterns, especially ivy.

Illuminated manuscripts of early Christianity were commonly decorated with simple leaf design. It is significant that some of the Pagan symbolism carried over into Christian ritual, and has remained a part through the years.

With Buddhism in the Orient there developed a dread of death. It seems only natural that offerings to the spirits should be of long-lasting evergreen foliage as a symbol of life.

THE ARRANGER'S INSPIRATION

Since it is apparent that Nature's talent for leaf design has always inspired artistic man, it is logical that their twirling, twisting, drooping, and upright patterns should challenge creative imagination in the arranger. Their wondrous shapes, hues, and textures, varied even with as small a thing as a shifting light or a change in the angle of vision, challenge close study.

There is need for this study for so far in arrangement, leaves have been accepted mainly as material of secondary importance—as background for or accompaniment to flowers. Perhaps this is due to the distraction caused by bright and varied hues in flowers, but once we are aware of the individual and intrinsic beauty in leaves, our aesthetic sense is satisfied with arrangements of foliage without flowers. A sensitive eye and mind will pilot you; the deeper you look, the more you will be impressed. And appreciation will be the start of action.

AWARENESS OF LEAF BEAUTY

I can't remember when I was not keenly aware of foliage. As a little child I delighted in picking up handfuls of autumn leaves which had fallen to declare the end of summer. I recall my avidity in pressing their beauty between the pages of a book. Fervor increased as scouting taught me to make blueprint pictures of their charm. The leaf of the maple tree held special thrill for me; something in its shape—a perfect pentagon around a point where diagonal veins meet, was irresistible. As I grew older, I enjoyed cutting its lovely shape into blocks of linoleum for eventual dye printing on silk. Today my pleasure in foliage represents the sum total of all early esteem, and explains my satisfaction in foliage arrangements.

Life is enriched by anything that kindles a spark of interest into fiery enthusiasm. I cannot say how your awareness to the arrangement possibilities in leaves will be quickened, but to study the trees in the changing seasons will help, should the thought be new to you. In their leaf formation, as in nothing else, Nature displays her tendency to design. Young, pale green leaves, lacelike against a cloudless sky of spring; lush green masses of summer's growth; a riot of coloration in the autumn scene; sombre brown leaves forming open pattern as they cling to bough of beech and oak when winter comes; the shape of each individual leaf echoing the shape of the tree as a whole—all this is a miracle of texture, hue, and shape.

THIS BOOK AND PURPOSE

To feel deeply about a thing is to want to do something about it—hence this book. Its purpose is not so much to guide you in designing unusual arrangements, as it is to encourage you to venture into a new field in the arrangement art.

A complete account of all possible foliage combinations is beyond the scope of this modest volume, and certainly such is unnecessary. A suggestive knowledge, as given here, should be enough to bring into focus the problem of knowing why some designs with leaves are pleasing and why some are not. Understanding will bring the whole phase to a category of easy "know-how".

3 AN INTERPRETATION: "Oh What a Beautiful Morning" is conveyed through the rooster and daisies, symbols of the dawn. Judiciously pruned nandina lends appropriate airiness. Backlighting strengthens the early-morning illusion.

ARRANGER: MRS. SHELDON BRANDENBURGER   PHOTOGRAPHER: DEWITT BISHOP

2

IN THE HOME AROUND THE YEAR

Your selection of foliage for a leaf grouping is a personal matter. You must consider what is available, its practical quality, and the purpose of the finished arrangement.

When flowers sleep in gardens during the winter months, arrangements need not be a luxury, nor should they present a problem for indoor decoration. No matter what the month or climate, or whether you live where you can share Nature's green earth, or as a "cliff dweller" in a city apartment, leaves are not denied you. A few are all you need to make a smart arrangement of long-lasting freshness and richness.

FROM THE FLORIST OR NURSERY

You can purchase greens at your florist or from your nurseryman's hothouse, and since they last so long, they are surprisingly economical. Many commercially grown plants have foliage without market value, for the public has not as yet been educated to appreciate it. This is a boon to the wide awake arranger. During pruning operations I have found nursery men happy to have me salvage leaves from their "clean up" practice. Lush, waxy, straplike greens from orchid plants, through just such means, have been the beginning of a dozen or more striking foliage combinations.

HOUSE PLANTS ARE A SOURCE

To be tantalized by things beyond immediate reach is a weakness in many, but the very wise will find satisfaction in avail-

4 FOLIAGE FROM HOUSE PLANTS
Three varieties of begonia are attractively combined. A strip of plumber's lead holds the branched stem in place.
ARRANGER: MRS. ROBERT A. VAN BOMEL
PHOTOGRAPHER: JOHN HUGELMEYER

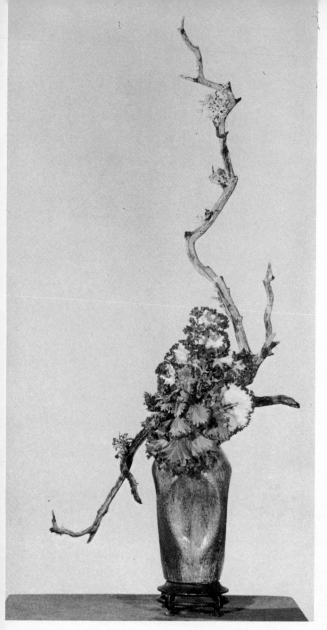

ing themselves of the easy to come by. A few blades, for example, pilfered from your house plants (Plate 4) or combined with gleanings from your yard can provide feature material for indoor composition.

PICK FROM THE GARDEN

The most logical source in the cold months is the needled and broad-leaved evergreen shrubs and trees. If you have a "seeing eye" there are other rich finds —English ivy, for instance, exhibiting a deep bronzy-green having been touched with frost (Plate 13). I have pushed aside the snow to find hollyhock leaves that have remained a lovely green in spite of the fact that this plant is among those flowering herbs which sleep under ground during the winter season. There will be other foliage awaiting your searching eye.

In our country's warm zone, almost any garden is evergreen with the amount of usable foliage so great that the problem is a matter of *selection* rather than of *seeking*. In the summer, of course, leaf variety in all gardens knows no bounds.

AT THE VEGETABLE MARKET

Unfortunately, not all of us have access to any of these sources, and we must

5 LEFT A SALUTE TO THE VEGETABLE KINGDOM On a dull black iron base, a handmade gray stoneware vase supports manzanita and kale in mauve and gray-green. Bits of moss carry the crinkly texture of the leaves to the comparatively smooth gray branch.
ARRANGER: MRS. MERRITT ENGLAND   PHOTOGRAPHER: C. G. BARNELL

6 FROM A SUMMER GARDEN In white porcelain with water a part of the design, a grouping of umbrella-plant (Cyperus alternifolius), saxifraga, dusty miller, and Christmas fern produces cool and refreshing images created by cutting back the leaf clusters of the umbrella-plant.
ARRANGER: MRS. HENRY BIRCHER   PHOTOGRAPHER: HOWARD OBERLIN

gather where we may. Vegetable gardeners will recognize the beauty of fernlike leaves of the globe artichoke, or the ornamental leafage of beets and carrots, or even the graceful vine of the edible pea, but you, without this source, can find lovely things in the vegetable market. I recall a prosaic spot in a home changed to one striking and gay with nothing more than curly, pale green leaves of cabbage combined with a lichen covered branch brought from the woods. In another interesting design, beet leaves with their dark red veining and bunched together, looked like a large exotic flower. And the handsomely ribbed leaves of the violet-red variety, and the exquisitely crinkled kale, are a joy to use. Even celery is interesting when it is combined with other leaves in arrangements.

and open mind to justly value common and familiar plants. And remember that today when arrangers go to great lengths to obtain exotic plants or those from far-away places, our commonplace greens become less common.

When we cut from the wild, we must be conservation-wise. Native plant growth, remember, is a natural resource of land protection and water regulation. Ruthless cutting and uprooting is a dangerous practice. Secure lists of those plants which can be picked without fear of extinction, those that must be picked with caution, and those that are protected by law against cutting, from your state's conservation department, or from the National Wildflower Preservation Society, or the National Wildlife Federation, both in Washington, D.C.

FROM THE WILD

Don't overlook the wildings or the so-called weeds. If it seems insensitive to bring their foliage to your attention, let it be realized that many have a particularly good quality and a character artistic enough for the most discriminating taste. There is something extraordinarily peaceful in a detailed and leisurely appreciation of humble growth. "To me the meanest flower that blooms can give thoughts that do often lie too deep for tears," said Wordsworth. His revelation is worthy applied to leaves; it may lead the receptive

UNEXPECTED SOURCES

Much that is lovely and unusual is concealed until an appreciative hand reveals it (Plate 10). In the heart of the variegated holly tree, you can find an ivory-white (sometimes with a pinkish cast), soft leaf growth sprouted close to the trunk. In the agave which grows so easily in our Southland, inner blades are waxen and of an ivory hue not matched by any other leaf; no harm comes to the plant when its heart is carefully removed. These leaves will turn in time to their normal green, but for weeks remain most un-

7 IN A BRONZE CONTAINER *Prunus ilicifolia, native from San Francisco to southern California, becomes contorted and ridden with moss and lichen when grown in sandy coastal areas. Seemingly dead, its tufts of tough, holly-like leaves prove that it clings to life.*
ARRANGER: FRANCES LOUISE BODE   PHOTOGRAPHER: WILLIAM T. BODE

8 ABOVE SPRINGTIME Flower buds and conspicuously-ribbed leaves of Hosta sieboldiana are simply and beautifully arranged in a swirl design.

ARRANGER: MRS. WILLIAM G. WHEELER   PHOTOGRAPHER: WILLIAM WHEELER

9 RIGHT ENTITLED "THE JANUARY STORY" In a gray-blue container on three circles of natural wood, dormant huckleberry is combined with hosta which has dried into interesting forms ranging in color from ivory to a deep tan. Vein pattern of the leaves harmoniously repeats line design in the branches and on the surface of the vase.

ARRANGER: MARGUERITE BOZARTH   PHOTOGRAPHER: C. FANDERS

usual. And the palm is fantastically twisted and corrugated in its unfolded development. This embryo palm can be purchased at your florist from commercially grown stock. Of course I do not recommend unthinking destruction of plants to obtain any material, but you are justified in using ·any part of a plant when a bulldozer invades a nature-planted area.

Even Nature's accidents can supply you with unexpected and distinctive foliage. I have seen a common pokeweed, because it was growing in the shade and so deprived of sun, a lovely chartreuse. On its violet-red stalks its foliage was something to exclaim about. At the moment of this writing, a potted philodendron on my desk carries three leaves so lacking in chlorophyll as to be a light cream-yellow. They mark the plant as having been neglected, but even so it has merit, for in these leaves I have something unusual to spotlight a foliage arrangement. How to cut leaves and branches without injuring the plant, to harden them for longer life, to treat with paint or varnish, to dry, to preserve them with glycerine, to skeletonize, and to force branches into early leafage is given in a coming chapter.

SEASONAL COLOR

In early spring, the earth becomes enlivened with the green of new growth. We need not be gardeners nor philosophers to rejoice with this yearly miracle of awakening. Truly, green is symbolic color in spring arrangements.

For the most part flowers in your summer garden wear the "hot" colors; there are few cool blues, violets, or even whites. When the thermometer soars, you can appreciate this lack of vivid color in soft tones of foliage hue. Not only do leaves last longer than bloom, but they add cool, refreshing atmosphere to your home (Plate 6). A starting point for a "cool look" can be bright and glossy greens in the empty fireplace in the manner of the English boughpot of leafed branches during summer days.

In autumn, Nature's replacement of her deep green mantel with fiery hues seemingly warming the chilly air is your cue to the special charm of fall arrangements. When nights grow cool, I know no lovelier sight than long colorful tree branches arranged effectively at the chimney side on the floor. Reflection of a cheery blaze brings out a beauty in the leaves you hadn't expected. Beautifully colored flowers of the tropics, vivid as they are, do not surpass the scarlet of the maples, the gold of the sassafras and the tulip trees, and the red of the oaks. Bright autumn leaves are peculiarly a possession of a colder clime; they deserve the best possible use made of them.

FOR THE FORMAL SETTING

A second step in the selection of foliage is to link up practical quality and availability of leaves with the setting your arrangement will occupy. If decorating the library is your problem, decide on the dignity and richness derived from an all green vertical plan (Plate 22). Sword-shaped blades, like those of iris or yucca, would be particularly pleasing for the backbone in a compact, stately design (Plate 24).

Perhaps you want eye-catcher decoration in an ultra-modern room where ornamentation is replaced with textural interest. This seems to demand decisive

10 UNEXPECTED BEAUTY A gall-infested locust tree offered the seeing eye this fascinating branch. It was pruned to produce a beautiful line and form pattern and supported in a pewter container. Green hosta leaves, Japanese bronze Obon dancers, and a black base complete this
lovely work.

ARRANGER: FRANCES LOUISE BODE   PHOTOGRAPHER: WILLIAM T. BODE

11 3-D ARRANGEMENT FOR A SHALLOW MANTEL SHELF With an overlapping of forms and shapes—sculpted heads, Cuban pineapples, anthurium foliage, and spotted house plant leaves—the arranger has created a strong sense of depth. Texture contrast is noteworthy.
ARRANGER: MRS. JOHN M. LANGENBERGER   PHOTOGRAPHER: U.S. ARMY PHOTOGRAPHER

shapes and solid forms to stimulate your desire to try for an appropriate structural effect. Nothing is superior to the succulents for this (Plate 27). Their fleshy forms range in texture and hue from waxy jade, through stony-gray, through porcelain and suedelike greens. Especially are the long leaves of the succulent sansevieria useful, for their trim lines harmonize with contemporary furniture (Plate 31). The cactus too, with its beauty sustained by surface texture, is especially fitting (Plate 30). Technically in this succulent specie, it is a spine covered or fluted stem rather than a leaf, which is usable in arrangement. In a sense, it functions as leafage, and so we are justified in considering its possibility in foliage groupings.

THE INTIMATE APPEAL

On the coffee table where a low arrangement is expected, leaves which are seen to advantage when looked down upon are the best choice. The wavey circle of the geranium (Plate 33) is a good example, as are the textured begonia blades, Plate 2. For those who have a glass top table which accommodates a support for an arrangement to be seen as you look down through the glass, there is nothing to surpass such a leaf grouping.

A mantel arrangement to frame a mirror or picture is shown in Plate 11. Also effective on the mantel is an arrangement designed low for use under a picture.

A hallway calls for a friendly, cheerful grouping (Plate 16). Here gay, variegated foliage is ideal. Or try for contrast in hue, such as in a red and green combination. Because contrast gives impact to attract the eye, it is superb to welcome

friends as they enter your home.

One of the especial joys of the day is to meet with family and friends around the dining table. Its decoration will be seen at close range, so choose foliage with special surface interest and hue. Plate 38 is suited to a breakfast nook.

You will not want to forget the kitchen where many of your household duties take place. Something lively and cheerful like an informal grouping of geranium leaves

12 SANSEVIERIA AND CUT LEAF PHILODENDRON *A bit of foliage and high aspiration makes this simple plan, tasteful in terms of today's standard.*
ARRANGER: MRS. ALFRED S. GRUSSNER
PHOTOGRAPHER: A. L. KNOWLTON

13 FROM A FEBRUARY GARDEN *Juniper, ivy, and sempervivum are arranged with a bare branch on a polished walnut plaque. St. Francis, patron of woodland creatures, in matching hues, adds a touch of religious sentiment.*
ARRANGER: MRS. A. B. ARRINGTON
PHOTOGRAPHER: LEW HENDERSON

will give you a lift. See Plate 35 for an appropriate idea.

Introduce glamour to your bathroom by hanging a wall vase, or a pair of them, carrying long-lasting arrangement of ivy tapering to tiny leaves on their sprays which hang over the edge.

A wall vase is useful in any room where table space is nil. It is an economy measure, too, since there is no need for leaves at the back; its design is seen only from the front and sides. In them trailing vines are particularly effective to direct the eye

14　IN OPAQUE GLASS　*Amaryllis, begonia, and variegated dracaena (calla lily type) arranged in a graceful Hogarth curve to match the smooth flowing lines of the glass bottle sprayed with gilt.*
ARRANGER: MRS. C. VERNE KLINTWORTH　　PHOTOGRAPHER: C. VERNE KLINTWORTH

15 SUCCESS IS A MATTER OF RELATIONSHIP *Yellow speckled aucuba leaves frame an ebony head on a mat of brown bamboo. Behind the figure three spotted stems removed from the rice paper plant (Tetrapanax papyriferus) at the base of its leaves add a quality of distinctive originality.*

ARRANGER: MRS. JAMES CASSIDY   PHOTOGRAPHER: MEL MANLEY

downward to a furniture grouping below.

By thinking in terms of your sense of smell, fragrance can add another dimension to arrangement. A bowl of scented leaves—pungent lemon verbena or spicy narrow-leaved rosemary, perhaps—on the bedside table is inducive to sleep.

In the sick room use an all green arrangement of delicate foliage to cheer a troubled heart. The beauty of quiet tones will never tire the shut-in's eyes.

The patio or porch can accommodate any low and heavy grouping in which design will not be spoiled through shifting in the breeze. If from this location you look out on a garden of green, you will enjoy color in contrast to the broad expanse of green background, so arrange some of the most colorful red or yellow leaves you can find.

And so we become aware that arrangements of leaves are appropriate and a delight anywhere in your home, and at any time during the year. And because of long-lasting attribute, they are a veritable time saver to the busy homemaker.

16 ELEGANTLY STYLED *An antique container of marble, bronze, and brass holds house plant foliage—yellow-striped pandanus and two varieties of variegated leaves in green and white.*
ARRANGER: MRS. F. PALMER HART
PHOTOGRAPHER: SEVECKE

3

THE ARRANGEMENT PLAN

A grouping of foliage, however, no matter how lovely each individual leaf, does not assure a pleasing arrangement. At every stage in the making, natural limitations of your medium determine both form and pattern of area relationship.

FORM, A RELATION TO PHYSICAL VISION

The structure of your eye is such that it demands form when elements of line, shape, hue, texture, and space are combined. Without it no complex subject can be comprehended.

A first step in achieving this is to compose within a three dimensional shape developed through the relation of solids (plant materials) and voids (spaces between) to a silhouette (boundary) implied by the extremities of the material used. For beginners, the form will be a geometric one, for there is a geometric basis to all things perceivable. This is not difficult to understand for it concerns the simple cube, sphere, and cone with their part forms, variations, and combinations allowing limitless boundary possibilities. Just which form and its size, is largely dependent on the arrangement's relation to its setting. For aesthetic pleasure it must fit comfortably into its allotted space which is bounded by a frame determined in various ways—by a window, a mantel, a table, a picture, or perhaps a wall niche. Harmony which comes through fitness of purpose is imperative, for no arrangement can be beautiful without it, no matter how well it is constructed, or how lovely its color or

17   IN THE SPIRIT OF HOPE AND JOY *Gentle natural curves in newly sprouted weigela branches impressed the designer with a feeling of joy in the fulfillment of resurrection. Arranged in a radiating pattern in a bamboo container, this composition would bring a touch of spring to any room.*

ARRANGER: FLORENCE M. SCHAFFER   PHOTOGRAPHER: MEL MANLEY

33

form. Whether the arrangement is large, medium, or small isn't important as long as its scale remains in accord with its surroundings.

LINEAR STRUCTURE HAS VALUE

A linear plan is required to establish form. You would find it most difficult to fit a mass of green leaves into a boundary without a definite skeleton. Structural and accented lines are predominating factors in setting its impression.

LINE DEFINES FORM

An appreciation of line, and form which it defines, is based on laws of human personality. This adds mood or symbolism to the arrangement. For example, gentle upright curves in Plate 37 express grace as opposed to the deep curviture, symbolic of exuberance even with a minimum of material, in Plate 11. Weary, downward curves in Plate 69 express an intended depression. Arrangements of a horizontal line structure would seem as peaceful as the quiet sea stretching out

18 LEFT DEPTH ACHIEVED *Just one leaf of iris and cranesbill, and two leaf-stems of lily of the valley are assembled in back, front, and middle planes.*
ARRANGER: MARGUERITE BOZARTH
PHOTOGRAPHER: C. FANDERS

19 RIGHT "BY THE WATER'S EDGE" *Cool in feeling is this naturalistic design. On a brown rock base, furrowed stems of the scouring rush (Equisetum hyemae), ferns, violet leaves, and undeveloped pine cones assume shelter for the green frog accessory.*
ARRANGER: MRS. LOUIS H. AMER
PHOTOGRAPHER: BEACON JOURNAL

20 EMPHASIS ON CONTRAST *In a white pottery "pillow vase," croton leaves and a trimmed sweet gum branch present stimulating impact of contrast.*
ARRANGER: HANS CHRISTIAN ANDERSON MADISON   PHOTOGRAPHER: JACQUES SAPHIER

to infinity, while a vertical direction (Plate 48) holds the dignity we associate with trees standing firmly erect against the law of gravity. A dominance of the diagonal direction, in recalling the slanted body of a running man, endows an arrangement with an impression of action. Plate 41 illustrates its use to strengthen an illusion of active freedom characteristic of the mighty falcon. In form, a pyramid firmly stationed on its broad base has steadfast and static quality founded in our instinctive enjoyment of stability and so fitting to religious sentiment (Plate 13). The angular boundary in Plate 50 sets the mood for the illusion of feeling intended by the designer.

PLAN FOR ORDER

Man dislikes a hodge-podge existence; he wants security. This desire is satisfied through an ordered plan in everything he does, including his artistic endeavors. Man is a thinking creature; he observes Nature's many lessons, but he is not content to display his observations haphazardly. Rather he controls them guided by natural laws, the fundamental principles, so that his effort results in oneness or unity of plan and purpose.

A good design is always a unity; its parts are so related as to enable you to "see the whole rather than its parts." This means that in the successful design, no element stands alone—each finds its rightful place in its extension in the allotted space. The word arrangement is synonymous with design and, as we already have established, order is required. This is accomplished in one of three possible ways or through the combination of them. The oldest and simplest of these is *repetition*, the combination of like

units. This mode respects a natural impulse due to our closeness to rhythmic repetition in breathing and in the beat of our hearts. In design, a repetitious pattern is obvious and uniform, and when carried to excess, may lead to a monotonous sameness which is detrimental to interest.

The opposite extreme is order through *contrast*, the combination of totally different units. If there is equally distributed opposition, however, there will be discord, and so disunity, in place of order and unity.

Midway between these two extremes is the order of *harmony*. This unites characteristics of both the other means in the combination of units alike in some respect, and different in another. Generally speaking, this is the most aesthetically pleasing unification because it represents agreement, required of unity, plus variety to prevent monotony of too much repetition.

All the plates in this book are illustrative of harmony with emphasis on one or another mode. Plate 57, for example, displays agreement of like and similar units with particular clarity. In Plate 55 harmony puts emphasis on repetition. In Plate 25 contrast is stressed.

VARIETY, A DEEPLY ROOTED INSTINCT

We can conclude that harmonious arrangement is simply a unified design which embodies some variation. That we all enjoy variety is evident in the oft-repeated phrase: "Variety is the spice of life." As in life, so it is in design, for art and life are closely allied.

It is because of variety that a curved line appeals to your aesthetic sense more than a straight one. The direction of the

latter is obvious, is without the subtlety which lies in the former through some variety in direction. For the same reason, we all agree that Hogarth's "Line of Beauty" pleases us more than the S curve from which it is derived. When the one-half circles in the compound S are elongated to become shallow curves in the Hogarth line, ratio is no longer constant; the curves are varied in their paths (Plate 14). Then too, in returning upon itself, the "Line of Beauty" shows variation in that one half is longer than the other; in the S, ratio is not only constant in the curves, but there is uniformity in their sizes as well.

PRINCIPLES OF ART

All principles work together to achieve order. One is as important as all others, is dependent on all others, and in turn is a result of all others. To separate them as individual factors is difficult, but, for the sake of study, I will attempt to do just this. The order of listing has no bearing on importance.

BALANCE

Keep the need for balance ever before you. In short, good balance involves a

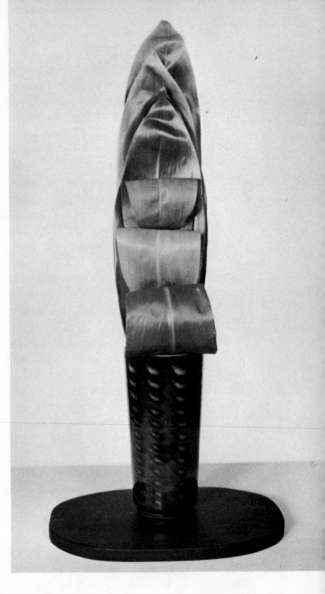

21 LEFT ASYMMETRICAL, WITH BALANCE BY PLACEMENT *As compared with the isosceles triangle (Plate 34), a left- or right-handed triangle is a freer and livelier conception. Here the base carries the eye across the design with the curve of a branch bringing interest to the open area to compensate for weight of material on the left of the central vertical axis.*
ARRANGER: MRS. JOHN W. KNIGHT, JR.   PHOTOGRAPHER: DWIGHT A. WALKER

22 ABOVE CURVED TO EXPOSE THE BACK MID-RIB *A vision charged with uniqueness yet ordered by a sense of fitness. Shape of the pheasant-eye Japanese porcelain suggests emphasis on the vigorous verticle pattern.*
ARRANGER: MRS. ALFRED S. GRUSSNER   PHOTOGRAPHER: A. L. KNOWLTON

proportionate relationship between the parts of your arrangement. Determine it by establishing a central axis line in your mind holding all parts of your design in equilibrium. Study Plate 29. You will see that the arrangement is stable—that is, it does not appear to lean to either side, forward, or backward, nor does it seem top-heavy. On the other hand, this stability prevents a squatty effect which would come with insufficient height of the plant material in the container. And so, each dimension of the plan has balance—perpendicularly (from the bottom of the design to the top), laterally (from side to side), and in depth (from front to back). See Plates 24 and 27.

More often than not, arrangers adhere strictly to a rule known as the one and one-half times measure for determining the height of an arrangement. This dictates that plant material be one and one-half times the height of a vase, or width of a bowl. But remember, it is effect, not rule, that should be uppermost in your mind. Among several examples shown in this book, Plate 18 is especially worth analyzing for height and balance. Here the proportion of plant material to container is considerably more than the usually accepted measure but it is artistically correct. As compared to the force of visual "weight" in magnolia branches, for example, lightness in the material of high placement, as well as a simplicity of detail, requires a greater than usual proportion of material to interrelate satisfactorily with the "weight" of the container.

There are two sorts of balance, symmetrical and asymmetrical. In the former, a vertical axis line (real or imaginary) divides the composition into like or similar halves. The symmetry need not be exacting (Plate 22). In fact, if exact repetition on each side of the axis is adhered to, uninteresting uniformity may result. Work for a similarity on both sides to maintain a feeling of symmetry, but plan for slight differences. Never forget that the essence of art is *repetition plus variety*; it is applicable to all types and styles.

In asymmetrical balance, there is equilization of interest or visual "weight," but not a regularity of repetition on both sides of the axis. In this sort, equilibrium can be, as always in symmetrical patterns, *self-contained* (the sum total of visual force on both sides is equal in attraction for the eye), or it can be achieved by *balance by placement*. With this means, one side is heavier than the other so far as plant material is concerned. Stability is gained by bringing enough interest to the open area (defined by boundary limitations) to compensate for that in the actual bulk of the design. Compare Plates 20 and 21. In both examples, unlike parts are held in balance by their pull on your eye, their attraction or visual tension, we might say. In this informal balance of inequalities, we find a subtle effect; balance is instinctively felt rather than obviously seen as it is in a formal, symmetrical design. If you are a beginner in arrangement, you will probably enjoy the static symmetry more than the dynamic asym-

23 TO UNDERSTAND THE WHOLE IS TO EXAMINE ITS PARTS *A distinguished composition described on page* 44.
ARRANGER: MRS. RAYMOND RUSS STOLTZ   PHOTOGRAPHER: BOUTRELLE-SEVECKE

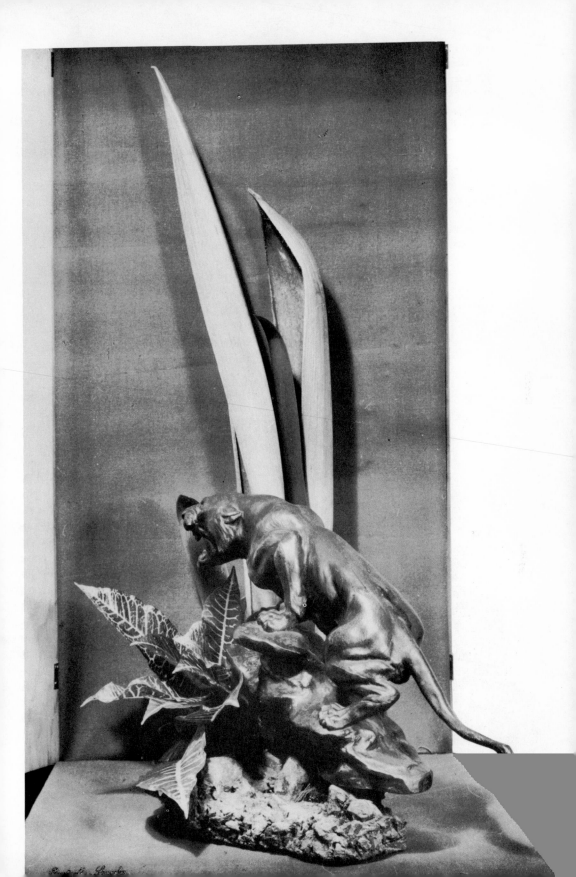

24 ANALOGY THAT STEMS FROM YEL-
LOW *Working from the background of stately
variegated yucca, green English laurel, and nested
green geranium leaves edged with yellow-orange
gives a solidity of pattern within the confines of
a static pyramid to express a personal significance,
titled by the arranger, "Quiet Reflection." Figure
and stone on which he stands echo these hues in
lighter values; the container is a grayed yellow-
orange.*

ARRANGER: MRS. MERRITT ENGLAND
PHOTOGRAPHER: C. G. BARNELL

metry, for it is not only easier to see,
but more easily achieved.

It is of interest to know that histori-
cally, asymmetrical balance is a later development in artistic expression. Unfortunately, there is no hard and fast rule to
guide you in a perfectly balanced relation
of the various units involved. You learn
to feel it instinctively if you school yourself to observe the harmony of balance in
all about you.

The impression of weight is all important. A dark green leaf, for example, is
"heavier" than one of the same size and
shape, but lighter in hue. In the same
way, a rough textured leaf appears to
weigh more than one of smooth surface.
In both cases, larger areas of the light
hue and of the fine texture would offset
smaller areas of the darker and rougher
foliage providing both were at the same
distance from the lines of balance (axes
lines). Shapes (and position, you will
learn) have bearing on eye attraction and
must be reckoned with. One curved line
can balance two straight ones because the
former has more appeal for the eye.
The key is in *interest.* An animated object, the tiger in Plate 23, for instance,
has more visual drawing power, because
of shape complexity, than would one in
a pose of rest. And so it is "heavier"
even though its hue, texture, and size
were approximately the same.

As to position, substance at the center
of gravity has less weight than that at
a distance from it. As the distance increases, so increases apparent weight. In
arrangement, respect this law of physics
by placing actual or apparently heavy
units low in the design, with the less
weighty (actual or apparent) toward the
top and edges of your plan as diplayed
in the various plates in this book.

25 A STUDY IN CONTRAST   In a black rectangular form, yellow-green New England flax in ascending pattern is intensified through supporting direction of a dark green horizontal plane of cotoneaster accented with a circular form of a red camellia in a black squarish container; the base is a black rectangle.

ARRANGER: MRS. JOE E. WOLFF   PHOTOGRAPHER: JOE E. WOLFF

PROPORTION AND SCALE

In definition we might say that proportion is the pleasing relationship of one part of a composition to another, and to the whole. It is closely allied to scale, but scale is a measure of size referring to individual parts such as leaves and container, while proportion has to do with the areas these units occupy. The size of the leaves in relation to the container is a matter of scale, while the amount of foliage in the container is a matter of proportion. For unity there is a need for unequal proportions. Equality in amounts in any areas would divide interest and so confuse the mind. With this lack of dominance there would be nothing more important than anything else to set the character of your plan. By way of example, if your design was equally divided between areas of round and spiked shapes, you could not determine whether it was a curved or an angular pattern. If it were equally divided between green and red, it would be neither a green design varied with red, nor a red design with green. An arrangement has pleasing scale relationship when there is a feeling of sequence in the size of area shapes, and satisfying proportions when there is a dominance in the distribution.

DOMINANCE AND CONTRAST

Dominance is a principle in its own right. One hue, one value, one texture, one shape, and one direction of line repeated often enough to become prominent in your design determines the character or intent of your plan. Examine Plate 23 for illustration. Here is a diagonal direction emphasized by the placement of the tiger and croton foliage. Unity is achieved

and monotony is prevented through variety supplied by the opposing direction in the skillfully subordinated coconut spathes. Even though this opposition is a stabilizing force in drawing the eye back from its path along the diagonal line thus preventing it from moving out of the frame of vision, it aids dominance too. By its very difference, or contrast (total opposition), it draws attention to the diagonal, emphasizing the impression of action. Success lies in the opposition being kept in subordination, and placed to carry the eye into the dominant feature.

Dominance and contrast, therefore, are problems of proportion bearing greatly on unity. Of the two principles, dominance is the end with contrast a means to that end.

In the example described above, the opposition is tied together through a concentration of interest in the area where the brightly colored croton leaves meet the dark of the figure's base. The impact is strong enough to pull the unlike parts together in rhythmic composition.

RHYTHM

When we speak of rhythm, we are getting close to the pulse of the design. Traditionally, the concentration of interest referred to above (generally called "center of interest") is the area from which all others derive their relationship; it is a magnet of unity, so to speak. A unified structure is one which as you look at it, is taken in (in its entirety) at a glance. Actually the lens of your eye does move, but if for the sake of order, you have grouped like shapes, like lines, like hues, like values, and like textures into areas

26 ASYMMETRICAL BALANCE, BY PLACEMENT *Color-marked leaves of the greenhouse grown maranta (prayer plant) highlight the evergreen pittosporum of a southern garden; the blotches match the hue of the bronze incense burner.*
ARRANGER: MRS. JOSEPH CORTESI   PHOTOGRAPHER: A. L. KNOWLTON

(Plate 21), and have distributed them so that your eye can travel in a natural radiating gradation (from large to small, dark to light, dull to bright, solids to voids as in Plate 13), there is a definite beginning and ending spot for your eye in the plan. When this happens, the one-glance illusion is strong, for there is no conscious change in the focus of your eye. Indeed, it is a physical fact that you can see an arrangement easily only if this point appears in your eyes' path through the plan's dimensions of height, width, and depth.

In arrangement this spot, known as the "focal point," becomes the nucleus of a center of interest area. The more complex is the pattern, the greater is the need for emphasis here where the lines in your arrangement meet as they rise from the container. Its placement is governed by an unconscious tendency to fix it in a correct relation to your physical vision. Be it noted that when the composition's center axis can be determined through the center of the vase or bowl (Plate 27), the center of interest is generally situated on it, just a little above the rim. If the vase or bowl is to one side of this axis (Plate 12), the center of interest moves to the left or to the right, at an area about one-third, more or less, from one side.

Thicken the plan at this point, or arrange color so that the greatest contrast of value and hue is here to attract the eye. Relate all line and mass shapes to carry it to this area. Voids in your silhouette are eye rest areas; plan even these to direct your eye here (Plate 42). In the successful arrangement, solids decrease in size from the body of the design to the extremities, while the voids increase in size.

The center of interest must be strong enough to support all that grows from it, so avoid a tight, pushed in effect. On the other hand, be careful that it is not too dominant. A "bull's eye" area would cause your eye to linger here. Keep in mind that it must move easily and immediately on through the design before it comes back to complete its circuit. Complete stoppage before this takes place would be distracting enough to necessitate a conscious change of eye focus; disunity would result.

Be careful to have only one center of interest visible at a time; there may be more in a free standing arrangement (one that is seen from any angle), but let there be only one to a side. There will be other minor interest points in your design certainly, for these may be needed to control movement, to bring repose to your plan. But to assure unity, let only one be dominant and, ideally, let it be an area including the natural focal point.

If you question how you can be sure to have a center of interest the most attractive part of your composition and yet kept only a part of the whole, I can only say with words of Shakespeare: "Aye, there's the rub." Ability takes practice.

27 SUCCULENT GRANDEUR *Repetition of scallops is a worthy note in this combination of kalanchoe and echeveria in a silver-washed copper urn. To retain color in a bronzy or rosy variety of echeveria apply water to the growing plant only if it seems to be wilting; water tends to turn the succulent green.*
ARRANGER: MRS. BONNIE C. PARSONS   PHOTOGRAPHER: C. VERNE KLINTWORTH

28 A BALANCED DUO *Beauty in a two-arrangement composition stems from the "little things." The placement and direction of Polydenium and Boston ferns and clematis in a wall niche, are among these small but important details.*

ARRANGERS: MRS. OLIVER A. VIETOR, MRS. GRAY MCW. BRYAN

PHOTOGRAPHER: JOHN HUGELMEYER

To be sure that you thoroughly understand rhythm, I summarize as follows: It is a major principle achieved through minor principles of repetition, gradation, radiation, and transition. Its aesthetic appeal is heightened through the minor principle of opposition.

PRINCIPLES IN UNISON

As stated earlier, success is accomplished through the combined efforts of all principles. No matter which you consider, its function is the same—that is, to achieve unity. If your finished product does not satisfy, check it over for the working principles. Either you have used one or more unwisely, or without full understanding. I am aware that it is easier to discuss the principles than it is to understand them. If at this point, full meaning has somewhat escaped you, be not dismayed; you will gain insight as you actually make an arrangement guided by Chapter 8.

4

COLOR AND TEXTURE

Because color is a positive emotional force in our lives and a strong contributing factor to texture, these elements are given emphasis in this chapter devoted to them alone.

Even though not all foliage is green, this hue is the usual and accepted color of leaves. This is natural since, for temperance sake, Nature unites the cool, calm quality of blue with the happy and lively character of yellow to produce the green of her vast background. When leaf-green is commonly described as a "dark blue-green," and it is accepted that the majority of leaves are green, it would seem that the designer of foliage arrangements is faced with a rather lifeless color effect. But such is not so. It is true that most leaves are in tones (neutralized hues) which means they lack full spectrum intensity. In my experience, the only leaf among the greens that matches the bright spectrum hue is that of the nasturtium. But the range that lies between leafage

only slightly grayed, as the white pine, and the almost completely grayed, as the field mullein, supplies the arranger with infinite subtleties of color. The movement from tone to tone it affords design, makes possible a color range as effective as that in the rainbow realm of flowers.

AS COLORFUL AS FLOWERS

When I think of foliage wearing a hue other than green, I conjure up a vista of autumn leafage. The green coloring matter, chlorophyll, in the summer blades has captured the energy of sunlight and, with magic it seems, has turned it to an exciting riot of crimsons, golds, and vermilions.

But at other times in the growing year there are "colored" leaves. Your observant eye will note a color difference between young foliage and the more mature on many border plants, shrubs, and trees.

29 EMPHASIS ON LINE AND FORM *In a wooden goblet on a cherry wood base, advantage is taken of the movement suggested in the gaily twisted and swirled desert pony tails and variegated red and yellow croton.*
ARRANGER: MRS. ALFRED S. GRUSSNER   PHOTOGRAPHER: A. L. KNOWLTON

30 STRUCTURAL QUALITY *The angled cactus, sun cereus (Heliocereus speciosus), is compatible with the sculptured piece, a truly modern interpretation of the mole. Repeating the rounded forms of its head and haunches, pinion cones prevent starkness. Use no water with the cactus arrangement as water hastens decay.*

ARRANGER: MRS. LAMBERT D. LEMAIRE
PHOTOGRAPHER: A. L. KNOWLTON

For instance, early peony growth is a deep, shiny red. Japanese andromeda has a superb coloring of burnished copper on its new growth. Young foliage on some of the wistarias could be matched to the light yellowish-brown hue of a baby deer.

And who among us will not respond with delight to the delicate beauty of golden spring leaflets on the poplar? There are lots of grays among the summer plants, especially on shrubs whose second name is *tomentosum*. In the border planting, artemisias are an especially lovely silver setting for surrounding greens. Don't overlook the golden privet, the maroon-red Japanese maple, and the giant kalanchoe which displays an overtone of orange.

And there is leafage that shows a difference of hue between the front and back of blades. Magnolia grandiflora is an example. It clothes itself in leaves which are smooth, dark bottle-green on the upper surface, and suedelike, reddish-brown on the underside. Banana shrub (Michelia fuscata) resembles a small magnolia, but its shiny leaves are lined with purple. Some leaves, as some of the fancy-leaved caladiums, have a contrast in hue between veining and the leaf's surface. There are multicolored leaves to be had—the crotons, for instance, that flourish in warm climates, and grow beautifully for me as a house plant.

In winter, we recall the crisp leaves in warm browns which still cling to beeches and oaks. And the evergreens so appreciated at this time of the year, are not all "forever green" as is generally supposed. When the temperature drops, some take on bronzy tones. Cryptomeria is an example; leucothoe is another. Mahonia changes to a deep purplish tone.

COLOR MANAGEMENT

Even though you rarely have to cope with intense hue when working with leaves, it doesn't follow that you have a limited chance for beautifully colored arrangements made just of foliage; combinations of subtle tones are often more satisfying than those of bright hues. In arrangements where leaves predominate, employ color as something to heighten effectiveness of design rather than in the narrower sense of fulfilling definite color schemes.

Just as the character of music is dependent on the pleasing variations of tone, and on the diverse transitions from soft to loud, so it is in color. Relationships follow the modes discussed in Chapter 3. Applying this to color, harmonize with areas alike in some respect, but different in another—all green, for example, but in a graded variety of value and/or intensity. The Japanese floral artists are masters in the use of values, often using those that are very close. Monotony is avoided through distinction resulting from the way the color cuts into the space in the Japanese tokonoma. Or gain drama with decided opposition in hue or tonal value arranged in accordance with your natural eye movement—green of Christmas evergreens, for example, accented with the bright red bracts (reduced leaflike organs) of the familiar poinsettia at the center of interest.

Study the plates shown in these pages for guidance. Note that a light or bright center of interest against a dark background of foliage, or vice versa, represents an effective tone distribution. This is one of the simplest means of interest stimulation in arrangement, but use it only in places where you want strong attraction, and even then in small amounts lest it be destructive to unity. Remember that the eye is drawn like a magnet to any area where opposition in any element meets. When you employ the means of eye impact at the center of interest, you

31 MODERNAGE For a T.V. room with black wrought iron furniture this stylized treatment of yellow-banded sansevieria accords with the triangular plastic container designed by the arranger. Its position on the base is distinctive and appropriate. Aralia with crassula (Chinese jade) at the base add a balancing factor.
ARRANGER: MRS. PATRICIA ULLMAN
PHOTOGRAPHER: DICK HAESELER

can prevent it from being over prominent by repeating it elsewhere in the design. Often it can coincide with an accent hue in an accessory.

Keep in mind the need for unequal proportions distributed according to the "law of area balance" which means that a large area of diluted hue (color lightened, darkened, or grayed) can be balanced by a comparatively small area of bright hue.

THE ELEMENT OF TEXTURE

Arrangements of leaves put emphasis on texture, a quality of immense aesthetic importance. It is determined by both your mind and touch, and is conveyed by structural substance, surface finish, color, pattern, and size. A texture is rough or smooth, dull or shiny, fuzzy or waxy, leathery or paperlike, open or compact, heavy or light, rugged or delicate, etc. In plant material it is a relative term, for a leaf is coarse or fine by comparison. A rhododendron leaf is coarse compared to that of the camellia; leatherleaf viburnum is coarser yet. The lance-shaped, tapering three-inch leaves of the black willow (Salix nigra) are comparatively more delicate than the larger five- to six-inch leaves of the weeping variety (S.babylonica), even though they have a similarity of substance.

Texture is so closely allied to color that the two can hardly be separated. Color tends to emphasize or minimize textural effect. By way of example, a blade of yel-low-green dieffenbachia seems delicate compared with a darker, all green variety.

HARMONY OF TEXTURES

Textures can be divided into two broad classifications: primitive and classic. Use together those that have something in common. For pleasing companionship consider a parallelism in those combined. Use rough with rough, and smooth with smooth, but remember the advantage of controlled variety to prevent a too tiresome repetition. There must be an underlying feeling of fitness in the diversity, however. The foliage of loquat with its impression of tensile strength is not in keeping with the comparative fragility of the lily-of-the-valley leaf. On the other hand, loquat and castor bean (Ricinus), while different in surface texture, have a common property of strength. As in line, in shape, and in color, use unequal proportions. Keep variation subordinated so as not to deprive the arrangement of character which, you recall, is always set by a dominant quality. See Plates 13, 30, and 32.

LIGHT MODIFIES COLOR AND TEXTURE

Color and texture of foliage is not a fixed item. The plant's age, where it is grown—in rich or poor soil, in sun or shade—is cause for change. As simple a thing as a cloud passing over your garden casting it

32 SUCCESS THROUGH TEXTURAL RELATIONSHIP Gray and brown dried yucca stems, brown Mexican Mezpah wood (tree gall or arboreal crests), aspidistra, and umbrella-plant (Cyperus alternifolius) are shown in a black Mexican container. Although the plant materials are arranged in a solid pattern, they maintain their separate characters because of their distinctive textures. Their common property is a sense of strength and substance.
ARRANGER: BERNICE KINNEY   PHOTOGRAPHER: WILLIAM T. BODE

into shade can modify plant hues and textures. Where just a moment before some foliage seemed bright in the sun, it is now darkened and dulled.

Shiny surfaces catch the light to give a sparkling distinction. Dark velvety-textured leaves like the Chinese velvet plant (Gynura), become completely characterless in shadowy recesses. Taking this into account, give your arrangement the advantage of the best possible lighting.

In a predominantly dark arrangement, only its silhouette will have importance if you place it against the light, as in front of a window. For best effect, put it where the light will come toward it or from above. Either way, the play of light on the points of recession will add an illusion of depth as well as reveal and enhance the design's color and texture.

On the other hand, foliage of a translucent quality is at its best if back lighted Calathea modeanna is a good example. When it is lighted from the front, the blade is opaque, but at a window with the light shining through, its beautiful veining is emphasized. It is little wonder it is commonly called "cathedral window."

You will avoid disappointment if you consider artificial lighting too, for most color and texture change under its influence. Light values tend to darken and the area narrows down; dark areas widen. Fluorescent lighting intensifies the cool blue-greens but deadens warm yellow-greens. The beauty of yellow-green foliage, on the other hand, is at its best when seen under the warm light of other types of artificial light, while cooler tones lose much of their richness.

COLOR RELATIONSHIPS

I have simplified the use of color and texture in foliage arrangement through the following summary of personal observation:

1. Use color considerably darker than spectrum green (including dark red, purple, all bronzy tones) to suggest shadow in the "heavy" areas of your design.
2. Leaves variegated with yellow, pale green, or white used in limited amounts in the "heavy" areas give a pleasing effect of dappled light likened to the play of sun filtered through a leafy canopy of trees.
3. Light green, yellow, or whitish leaves can brighten an arrangement. Use them generously in shadowed corners of a room.
4. A touch of bright hue will often transform a characterless grouping to one of richness. Pale hues without it may seem "over sweet"; darks, over drab.
5. Yellows, oranges, and crimson-reds lend a warm gaiety to a plan.
6. It is a fact that when we look at the so-called warm hues (yellow, orange, red) and cool hues (blue-violet, blue, blue-green), a change in the lenses of our eyes is responsible for their apparent movement, with the warm hues advancing, the cools retreating.

33 A MERRY NOTE FOR THE BREAKFAST TABLE *Variegated geranium leaves and brown rocks in yellow-lined brown pottery.*
ARRANGER: MARGUERITE BOZARTH   PHOTOGRAPHER: C. FANDERS

Color affects depth perception according to its warmth and its intensity. A blue-green of the same intensity as a red will recede, while the red appears to advance. But if the blue-green is more intense than the red with which it is combined, the reverse is true—the blue-green advances. A rosy-hued leaf is warm against a soft green, but cold next to a burnt sienna.

7. Any hue next to a stronger and more intense one becomes grayed by contrast. Large areas of white tend to dull dark green almost to making it seem dingy. A small amount of white, however, with lighter greens, deepens the tone to richness.

8. The impact of contrast in value or hue makes an arrangement seem nearer than it is. Use it when the plan is to be seen from a distance.

9. Very grayed foliage, as the blue spruce, does wonders in an illusion of depth.

TEXTURE RELATIONSHIPS

1. Smooth and shiny foliage reflects light to make its hue appear brighter and livelier. The grayer the hue, the rougher the leaf appears to the eye.

2. Shiny surfaces give emphasis to shape and form; rough surfaces have considerably more power to blend.

3. Hard, shiny textures have a pull on your eye and so seem nearer than dull, rough surfaces. A discreet combination can aid depth perception.

4. In an arrangement dominantly darker than spectrum green, some glossy texture will avoid a too heavy effect.

5. Leaves that reflect light add pleasing highlight to design.

6. Texture is effective through contrast. Shiny leaves make dull and dark foliage look deeper and darker by contrast.

7. Feathery leaves have soft textures and help to blend sharp outlines.

34 WITH A TOUCH OF NOSTALGIA *Americana implied by the old wooden mortar and pestle sets the tone in a family room designed for casual, countrified living. Yellow-edged sansevieria gives height; clustered bronzy galax leaves, body; dark green yew and bronzy mahonia, transitional interest.*

ARRANGER: MRS. JOHN W. KNIGHT, JR.   PHOTOGRAPHER: DWIGHT A. WALKER

5

CONTAINERS, STANDS, AND ACCESSORIES

CONTAINERS

The most satisfying designs appear controlled without a forced or stilted effect. The container is but a part of the whole and in traditional work holds subordinate role. It is, nevertheless, a vital instrument in success, with its size, its shape, and its character of such import that your selection is not something indifferently carried out. In general, the simpler the container, the easier it is to use.

SIZE

Just as scale or size relationship between the leaves combined in the container is important, so it is between the leaves and the container. Your eye would be distracted if it looked upon the tiny foliage of boxwood in a massive receptacle, or upon large canna blades in a small, five-inch vase. Scale must be just right to insure harmony. It must be right too for the amount of foliage placed in it. Proportion, you will recall, is a matter of judicious balance between the amount of leaves and the container. One that is too small will make the arrangement appear top heavy. One too large will, by subordinating the leaves, be emphasized to dominance which is contrary to sought for effect in traditional design.

SHAPE

Choose a container of such contour that foliage seems to "grow" with natural freedom from it (Plate 37). How to decide on its shape is implied in Aesop's fable concerning the fox and the stork. Each creature was unsuccessful in consuming food supplied in a receptacle designed especially for his rival's particular manner of eating. Suitability, we can conclude, is a first requirement for success.

Choose a container of a shape consistent with the planned-for design pat-

35 AN ARRANGEMENT WHILE FOLIAGE ROOTS *A spicy note for any corner in the kitchen is this salt cannister in which cuttings from house plants (Tradescantia fluminensis or wandering Jew, Annona reticulata or bullock's eye, and spiny-toothed Aloe ferox) seem at home while they root in water.*

ARRANGER: MRS. LAMBERT D. LEMAIRE   PHOTOGRAPHER: A. L. KNOWLTON

36 ABOVE A DIGNITY TO PLEASE THE MOST SEDATE A bronze suiban is harmonious in quality and sufficiently substantial to carry the strong bold silhouette of strelitzia foliage with the focal area of fancy-leaf philodendron.

ARRANGER: MRS. ALFRED S. GRUSSNER   PHOTOGRAPHER: A. L. KNOWLTON

37 RIGHT DESIGNED FOR COOLING EFFECT Pilea, philodendron, nephthytis, and sansevieria are combined to suggest the natural growth of these plant materials. An effect of coolness is achieved with water as an integral part of the composition. It is emphasized by the blue-green lining of the container.

ARRANGER: MRS. ALDRICH BLOOMQUIST   PHOTOGRAPHER: GOPHER STUDIO

tern, and with the arrangement's purpose. If it is to fit into a shallow space, select a bowl or dish-type receptacle, but one deep enough that the water it holds will come well up over the stem ends. If it is to be tall, use one with an opening large enough to prevent crowding the foliage.

Examine this book's illustrations to see that the most harmonious arrangements are those in which character, color, line, and shape recur in likeness and variation. You would be displeased with wide-spreading branches in a tall narrow container, for the expansion would seem forceably inconsistent. A bowl or oblong container would allow a natural freedom to the spread.

If your vessel has swelling sides, repeat its leading lines in the leaves. To illustrate, delicately curved branches of Scotch broom giving height to mountain laurel foliage would relate well to a spherelike bowl; large structural blades curving in outline as in the canna, would be a suitable background for rhododendron in a vase with curving contour; stiff, straight-edged leaves of yucca combined with triangles of some of the rex begonias would fit comfortably in a stright sided container. Note especially the harmonious shape relationship displayed in Plates 5, 37, and 54.

The classical urn seems to demand a more formal arrangement than does a cylinder or rectangular shape. The "high bowl" or standard-type is a particularly striking choice for it "sets off" the plant material in much the same way as a pedestal does a sculptured piece (Plate 29). A favorite standard-type among arrangers is the handsome iron "Cash Po." These were tops on the early 19th century parlor Franklin stoves. Originals, copied from French designs, are hard to find, even where antiques are sold, but foundries are reproducing them today thanks to the arrangers' interest.

With the "heavy" mass of foliage coming high in such a plan, it accords with the growth principle in Nature which shows plants rising up to wear a crown of bloom, like the crown imperial, above a low, small cluster of foliage. Then, too, this chalice-type gives opportunity to use trailing vines in graceful pattern. When foliage is arranged in a low container, it gives more weight at the base as we find it in the more general growth plan of a single flower rising above a clump of foliage (Plates 6, 8). The rectangular Chinese "pillow vase" is versatile. Almost any pattern is at home in it.

CHARACTER

For harmony, a container's inherent quality must agree with that in the foliage. Ideally, sturdy types of heavy pottery, wood, and metal suit rugged growth, while the more refined pottery, porcelain, alabaster, and glass satisfy the more delicate. Much of character depends on actual or apparent weight which is influenced by texture, color, and surface pattern as well as size and structural sub-

38 GOOD RELATIONSHIP *In a green and white chocolate pot of French pottery, new yellow and red crinkly leaves of rhubarb and irregular deeply indented artichoke leaves highlight a grouping of castor-oil plant, pittosporum, philodendron, and Pelargonium fragrans. The cup is a logical accessory.*

ARRANGER: MYRA M. MATHERS   PHOTOGRAPHER: JOHN HUGELMEYER

stance. For example, because in pottery, texture is largely in its glaze, a finely glazed piece will seem more fragile and so can carry "finer" foliage than one finished with a coarse glaze or none at all. Pandanus is at home in a glossy, smooth surfaced container; podocarpus is pleasing in softly semi-glazed pottery; loquat suits the coarser pieces. Thickness of the substance from which a container is fashioned is emphasized by surface pattern, and has influence. One of clay decorated with strong and definite design such as we see in much Indian and Mexican ware is "heavier" and "coarser" than one of the same thickness, but with unpatterned surface.

COLOR

Color too is a consideration—the darker it is, the heavier the container appears to your eye. Particularly in glass, color has strong bearing. When darkly colored, it seems of more rugged structure than clear or just slightly tinted glass. Consequently, it can hold "coarser" foliage than the latter. The delicate and slightly yellowish foliage of Rosa hugonis would be subordinated if used in a dark vessel, but in pale amber glass it would hold its rightful place.

You will find arranging in glass more difficult than in an opaque container because of an added problem of stem design. I advise the beginner in arrangement, if she must design in glass, to render it opaque by adding a little milk to the water. Bluing, vegetable coloring, or colored ink added to the milky water gives color if you desire it, and will not be harmful to the foliage. Plate 14 shows glass camouflaged with paint. Just how to achieve balance below a container's rim is discussed in Chapter 11 devoted exclusively to the challenge of arranging in glass.

Getting back to color, there will be harmonious relationship if the container's hue is brought into the foliage design (Plate 16). A bit of the yellow spring or fall foliage of buroak (Quercus macrocarpa) carries out the color of brass; dried leaves of sun flower or aspidistra echo copper, and alba poplar accords with silver. Containers of dull metal, bronze, or wood are appropriately related to the tones of foliage that is dried. Bronze is effective with the brown of heavy branches. Pewter is good with gray wooly textures like mullein. Pottery with a bronzed-green glaze comes close to perfection when used with a green leaf grouping. The use of white and black, even though these are neutral, is comparatively limited. A white container will satisfy only in an arrangement that carries a dominant amount of very light value in leaves (and such are rare). A black one relates well only if the foliage used with it is predominantly dark.

Your choice of color in vase as well as foliage depends to a large degree on where you plan to stage your finished product. For good, all around use, a gray container will serve you well. Since most foliage is

39 ELEGANCE THROUGH QUALITY *Aspidistra and variegated dracaena curved and looped for drama in an alabaster bowl.*
ARRANGER: MRS. HERBERT WOOLF, SR.   PHOTOGRAPHER: C. VERNE KLINTWORTH

40 LO . . . THE NEW AND THE OLD *Here are clearly defined textural areas and a fine relation of dark and light tones in fresh, greenish-yellow fringed bamboo; red-violet veined and hooded, elongated trumpet-shaped leaves of the pitcher plant (Sarracenia); gray-green kalanchoe covered with a coppery fuzz; and antique wooden Siamese temple figures, rubbed with yellow-green. The split bamboo textile in the background inspired this unusual composition.*
ARRANGER: ZELDA WYATT SCHULKE   PHOTOGRAPHER: JULES SCHICK

41 TO EMPHASIZE A MUSEUM REPLICA *From the collection at the Cloisters (New York) the bronze falcon replica stands free in symbolic composition. Contrasting textures in a variety of hosta and begonia foliage echo line and form. Golden-brown and gray rock formation and gray moss add textural interest. At the center of interest, hoods of skunk cabbage, dried to a gray-black hue, repeat the curve of the great bird's beak.*

ARRANGER: MRS. CLIFFORD E. CYPHERS   PHOTOGRAPHER: WIDE WORLD

grayed to some extent, it fits well not only with the container's neutral value, but with the home's decoration which for the most part is in softened tones. Incidentally, gray is foolproof with grayish foliage.

TREAT YOUR CONTAINER TO SUIT

It is a simple thing (and fun!) to disguise the color and texture of a container to better suit its environment. Perhaps the white of a cherished alabaster urn is out of character with the color in your home. Remedy this by tinting it with a wash of water-color paint. Remember though, the color will be there to stay. No amount of washing can remove that which has been absorbed into the cracks or "veins" of the alabaster.

Inexpensive pottery often crazes which is helpful in giving it distinctive treatment. Rub over its surface with burnt umber just as it is squeezed from the tube. The paint sinks into the minute cracks and when the surplus is wiped away with a soft cloth, you will have a container to rival the finest crackleware.

Pottery may be "antiqued" by boiling it in strong tea. Pearl-gray or leaf-green water paint rubbed with a soft cloth into the surface of a wooden receptacle results in a handsomely aged finish.

If your container is too shiny, dull it by applying condensed milk by means of a sprayer. Or try a coating of liquid wax. It tends to dull those surfaces to which it will adhere. Dull copper with liquid ox-blood shoe polish.

SHINY CONTAINERS

I do not mean to imply that the shiny surface is taboo. Often it can be the very thing for a certain setting. Old metal, for instance, burnished to a soft gloss will be beautifully harmonious with rooms in pale hues. But the reflection of light on a highly polished surface can sometimes prove troublesome. Lovely and shining silver, brass, or copper will delight you in a shadowed corner, but in bright light their elegance can be obscured. If the light is strong and direct it may cause highly polished surfaces to mirror surroundings to such extent that you see reflection from windows or lamps rather than the container's color and texture, and in fact, shape. When this happens, stability is effaced. On the other hand, a soft luster on a metallic surface can bring out reflections but to a lesser degree and without hiding color, texture, or shape. In fact, softly reflected light may emphasize a container's form.

GOOD DESIGN HAS NO PRICE TAG

A collection of good containers doesn't mean costly or rare possessions. Of course, such would be a joy to own, but they are not necessarily synonymous with good taste. You can purchase many well designed vases and bowls at nominal cost. A simple inexpensive basket, for example, offers innumerable and attractive possibilities. Its color, and its ruggedness or delicacy of weave, will guide your selection of leaves arranged in it. Baskets re-

42 THE MODERN TENDENCY TOWARD CONTRAST *Podocarpus, croton, and gera-nium leaves give contrast in shape, texture, and pattern in a contemporary ceramic vase.*
ARRANGER: MRS. LAMBERT D. LEMAIRE   PHOTOGRAPHER: A. L. KNOWLTON

quire a lining to hold water—an inserted bowl will do. Or fashion a lining from kitchen aluminum foil.

An ardent arranger is always on the watch for new and unusual containers. But one thing is sure—it is foolhardy to purchase one simply because you greatly admire it without consideration as to how well it will meet your need. I am intimately acquainted with such error and, as a result, my shelves hold lovely containers I have never used in my home with complete satisfaction.

Of course in any home there are receptacles not intended to hold cut plant material. Even a dump heap offers possibilities. I have retrieved a sea-green glass bottle that is the envy of my friends. It brings out the beauty of almost any foliage I use in it, and it is a constant source of pleasure. And there is always Nature's supply—pieces of weathered wood, shells, for examples.

Or for an inexpensive container, try your hand at making one. One of the loveliest foliage arrangements I have ever seen was a combination of dried banana leaves in a boxlike affair made of four pieces of natural plywood fed with an oil base furniture polish. An exquisite, soft luster finish resulted, to echo the hue and the smooth kid-glove texture of the magnificent foliage. An ingenious homemade container is shown in Plate 51; you will think of others.

STANDS

One cannot consider containers without thoughts of stands or bases which can add so much attractiveness to an arrangement. You may employ one for a variety of reasons. It may bring better balance to your plan or add height to the container for more pleasing proportion. In this "setting off" function, the base seemingly lends added importance to the arrangement. But stands have a practical quality too in protecting a bare table top from scratching or from moisture rings deposited by an inevitable "sweating" of a container not properly glazed on the bottom.

HARMONIOUS RELATIONSHIP

When you realize that the origin of the stand is the curve of the foot and the instep, you will understand its proper relationship; it must be right in size, in shape, in hue, and in texture. Determine size by the role the base will play (Plate 40). Its shape should harmonize with that of the container (Plates 5, 83). A dark stand of teakwood, mahogany, or walnut will satisfy in most cases. An ebony textured wooden base lends formality to an arrangement and is a wise choice with "refined" containers (Plate 27). Under a receptacle of "crude" texture such would be unfitting; an unfinished wooden plaque would be a more harmonious choice.

Most stands are made of wood, but you will find those of other materials intriguing. Slate, stone, marble, bark, cork are possibilities—in fact, any thing that

43 GAY IN SPIRIT *On a pine board (finished by hand rubbing) weathered wood, fresh oak leaves, and acorns give atmosphere to complement an amusing ceramic bird — like the wise old owl which an old poem tells us, "sat in an oak."*

ARRANGER: MRS. SHELDON BRANDENBURGER
PHOTOGRAPHER: DEWITT BISHOP

can serve as an attractive and substantial base is usable. Plate 71 shows a shallow bowl used upside-down as a base.

Among my treasured bases, a hand-cut and hand-polished burl has frequent use. To make one, obliquely saw (or have sawed) a plank from a tree stump that has weathered in sun and storm. Cherry, hard maple, or oak are exceptionally good because of their interesting grains. (Plate 44 displays a base with its grain pattern used to emphasize a theme). Thickness depends on the size of the stump which automatically determines the length and width of the finished piece. Wrap sandpaper around a block of wood for easy handling, and use this to sand both sides to smoothness. Then coat with clear varnish. When it has dried thoroughly, rub it down (with good hard elbow grease) to a satin finish. Plate 43 illustrates such a base.

It is reasonable to assume that you cannot have a stand for each container you possess, but a few oblong wooden plaques will prove versatile and will be suitable for many arrangements. I use liquid shoe polish to cover scratches—black on black, brown on walnut, and oxblood on mahogany. Furniture polish designed for blond woods conditions natural wood bases.

PLACEMENT ON THE STAND

A variety of compositions well placed on oblong stands are shown in Plates 3, 10,

22, 48, 51, and 83. Note the unifying value of that in Plate 13, where the interplay of the arrangement and accessories is satisfactorily complete on one common base.

ACCESSORIES

According to the dictionary an accessory is something which "aids in a subordinate way." An accessory can sometimes be used to advantage in arrangement. It can continue an effect of line (Plates 19, 46), bring out color or texture (Plate 17), secure perpendicular balance through emphasis at the focal area (Plate 15), or satisfy lateral balance through placement beside an arrangement (Plates 10, 13).

In a naturalistic design as pictured in Plate 47, a figure establishes an important sense of scale. In any arrangement it can help in "telling a story." A bird with outspread wings suggests a theme of flight and would be appropriate in a dynamic pattern; in a pose of rest it would suit a more static design. A reclining deer indicates tranquility; a Victorian paper weight "picks up" the spirit of a past era, while a sculptured piece of ultra-modern character would set the tempo for contemporary expression.

CHOOSE AND USE WITH THOUGHT

Choose accessories with an eye to color, texture, size, and shape as well as story-

44 A STORY-TELLING ARRANGEMENT *A plank charred and hand-rubbed to make its circular grain prominent adds to the theme of this bit of make-believe. Because the eye seeks things that are alike, these curves start the search for others of its kind easily found in the graceful ivy sprays and the duck accessories. Galax gives body weight; silver-spotted begonia gives a warm and exciting climax to steady the whole.*

ARRANGER: MRS. JACK R. CAMPBELL   PHOTOGRAPHER: ROCHE

telling quality. Exercise the same understanding you employ in selecting your container. Plate 56 shows an accessory chosen with sympathy for color, texture, shape, and subject of the vase with which it is used. In Plate 47 the arranger has chosen her plant material to maintain a pleasing scale relationship with the figure which sets the mood.

The proportion of the arrangement to one or more objects depends on the effect you want. If the object is to be an accessory, subordinate it to comply with the meaning of the word. On the other hand, it is possible to reverse this usual procedure to give prominence to a choice objet d'art with the plant grouping playing an accessory role. The idea for the interpretive design in Plate 41 was released by the lovely figure and so its dominance is warranted. Deliberate emphasis of the falcon was attained in an elevated position. In Plate 45 the arranger has exercised a truly seeing eye in her choice of objects combined with plant material—result of disaster has become element of artistic design.

PLACEMENT OF ACCESSORY

As to the position of an accessory in relation to an arrangement, there is no specific rule; several things contribute to success. One is size. If the accessory is too large, it will become more than a part of the composition. If it is too small, it will be dwarfed to insignificance which renders it meaningless and so superfluous to the design. If large-scale makes the accessory obtrusive in contradiction to your plan, push it farther back in the design to lessen its importance. Reverse the picture and compensate the too small object by giving it the advantage of forward placement to increase its importance.

If an arrangement is to share a table or mantel with objects such as books, ash trays, a candle stick, or figurine, perhaps, place the objects so that they direct your eye to the arrangement. Otherwise the accumulation of unrelated articles will draw attention from the arrangement.

This factor of eye psychology is important in determining placement. If an accessory is to contribute to the whole, your eye must be able to include it easily in its rhythmic passage through the composition. Because directional movement of an object carries the eye, arrangers generally place a figurine to look at or move into the arrangement (Plates 13, 17). But such practice is not law. A figure can be successful pointing away from the arrangement providing it has plenty of space to look or move into, and something in this space to catch the eye and through the illusion of movement, throw it back into the arrangement, thereby keeping it within the frame of vision.

A third consideration in unified placement is a sense of fitness. In a low container, an aquatic loving animal has a logical relationship when placed in the water, but for unity of idea, keep a land creature out of it—elevated on a stone, perhaps, or set apart from the arrangement.

45 A FANTASY IN ARRANGEMENT *Intense heat from a fire caused plastic garden hose to drip into weird blackened forms suggesting "ghost goblins" to the arranger. Budded trumpet vine and young fern fronds complete the grouping on black obsidian.*
ARRANGER: MRS. JOE E. WOLFF   PHOTOGRAPHER: JOE E. WOLFF

NATURAL ACCESSORIES

Often an accessory is a man-made object, but Nature offers interesting shells, stones, knots of wood, gnarled roots, fungi, and the like, yours for nothing more than the time it takes to gather them from her beaches, in her woodlands, and along her byways. Natural objects have a special affinity for plant material. I think the reason these gifts of Nature are so enjoyed is that we ourselves are governed by the same forces that shape their existence.

I prefer weathered wood pieces in their natural gray patina—with no treatment other than a washing and a whisking away of loose and rotted particles with a wire brush. Even to wax the surface removes the silvery patina of weathered wood. However, you may wish to change hue and texture for a particular problem; it is easily accomplished. Simply apply a wood stain, an oil, or a wax finish.

BACKGROUNDS

In a sense, a background against which an arrangement is staged, is an accessory. The term itself suggests something which "aids in a subordinate way." But at the same time, a well functioning background shows off an arrangement to its best advantage.

Use a simple one-hue plan against a patterned wall, less competition be as though the principle of camouflage had been deliberately applied to disguise the arrangement's design. If you favor an especially complex pattern in your plan, free it from a confusing background with a suitable tray or disk of wall board as in Plate 15. Against a plain wall setting, keep in mind that with dark against light, or light against dark, you can more easily distinguish the interplay of area shapes that make up the composition's pattern. When the tonal value of an arrangement is too close to that of its backdrop, its design is absorbed to such extent that it loses its identity of silhouette; it will appear flat and uninteresting.

TO USE OR NOT TO USE

No matter what you choose as accessory, be sure it contributes definitely to the idea you have in mind. If you are sure that it does, use it by all means. If not, omit it. Arrangers have a valuable slogan: "When in doubt, leave it out." Simplicity is always a virtue; it is far better to refrain from using accessories than to incorporate something that competes with the arrangement for attention. When you do include one in your design, let it definitely subordinate or dominate; competition weakens rather than beautifies.

My advice is to be sparing with accessory ornaments; an effect through the dramatic nature of the foilage itself is, after all, the most satisfying plan.

46 TO SUGGEST LIFE IN THE SEA *Green-veined marble, transparent green "bubbles" and glass fragments, a clear glass fish, driftwood colored gray-yellow-green, begonias showing soft-toned red undersides, and grayed green of sempervivum give color and form appropriate to the theme.*
ARRANGER: MRS. VINCENT DAIGLE   PHOTOGRAPHER: AL ALLEMAN

47 "HE LEADETH ME BESIDE STILL WATERS"   In a shallow receptacle an Oriental figure sets a natural scale for this interpretive work. Careful pruning produces "tree" and "grasses" besides the "still waters." Stones conceal mechanics and add to the theme.
ARRANGER: MRS. JOSEPH J. WAECHTER   PHOTOGRAPHER: C. B. SMITH-FLO. D. SMITH

6

HOW TO CUT AND TREAT FOLIAGE

There is a proper way to cut foliage and branches. In general, pick leaves early in the morning or in late evening when the plant tissues are firmed with moisture. Gather branches for fall coloring just as the leaves begin to change their hues. They will drop almost at once if they are left too long on the shrub or tree. If you cut them early in the season, richness of tone will develop in the vase and they will remain fresh and lovely for many weeks.

CUT WITHOUT INJURY

For future beauty and growth, it is important that neither the plant nor its appearance should suffer. But don't hesitate to cut from even your most valuable garden shrub or tree, for *careful* pruning is not injurious. In fact, done properly, pruning gives renewed vigor to the plant, and can improve its shape. In cutting, keep the following recommendations ever in mind:

1. Visualize the placing of a branch in your arrangement so as not to cut more than you will require.
2. Use sharp pruning shears—never tear off the branch as the resulting jagged break invites decay.
3. Bend the twig toward you and cut backward on a slant above a node or bud—not so close as to injure the bud for this is embryonic of a shoot to come, but not so far above it that you leave an unattractive nubbin.
4. Never cut a leader branch; its removal

48 "STATUESQUE" *In stately polished willow wood, vigorous pussy willow twigs with swelling buds meet succulents and English laurel leaves in clarity of design befitting the arranger's interpretation of her title.*

ARRANGER: MRS. DALE HUDSON   PHOTOGRAPHER: C. G. BARNELL

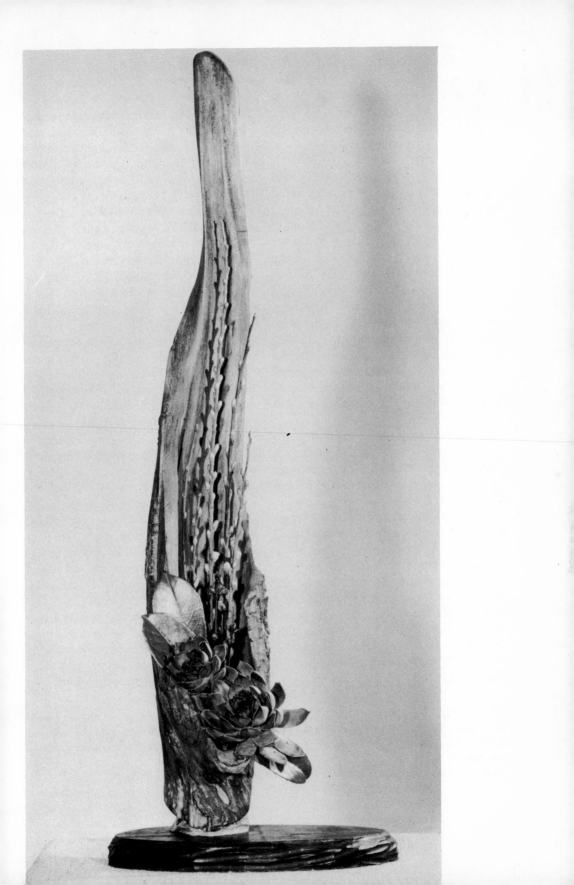

will give a stunted look to the plant. On slow growers, cut from the sides of the branches rather than the tips; gather from varied places to protect the plant's symmetry.

In gathering leaves from bulbs and corms, be sparing in the number taken from each plant, for removal of foliage is detrimental to the next season's bloom in proportion to the percentage of foliage removed; not more than one-sixth of the total leaf area should be severed. Pull off, rather than cut, the foliage. You will find with some bulbs, the narcissus is one, that the leaf is whitish toward the base. Remove this by cutting into the green to enable the blade to take up water. The cyclamen foliage, when it is pulled from the cormlike tuber, tends to curl at its base. This too must be cut off so the leaf can drink its fill.

One would think there was nothing to gathering ivy, but a few suggestions, if followed, will reward you. If you cut these leaves in freezing weather, immerse them in *cold* water when you bring them indoors. Let them remain here at least until the water reaches room temperature. If you desire upright sprays, gather those that grow upward on a tree. Slip a knife blade between the ivy's stem and the tree's trunk moving it gently up and down to lift the spray without its breaking. Incidentally, this is considerably easier to do on a rainy day.

To lighten or heighten the hue of leaves, wash them in sudsy water.

CONDITIONING

The Orientals, who are masters in prolonging life in cut plant material, use many and varied conditioning treatments. A different one is suggested for almost every type of plant. For the arranger of leaves, however, either one of two practices (soaking stems or soaking leaves) is adequate. The important thing is to encourage the foliage to absorb enough water to stimulate leaf tissue. You can keep well conditioned foliage nicely in the hydrator of your refrigerator. This is an asset if you wish to hold leaves for a later use.

All freshly cut leaves benefit from complete submergence in water. In fact, some will wilt immediately unless the entire leaf is soaked for several hours before arranging. Bamboo, the new spring growth of the climbing rose, of peony, and of maple fall into this class. Canna foliage is temperamental, sometimes lasting well without complete submersion. But it is certain that you will not be disappointed if you take this added precaution to insure its crispness. Cut palms often fold up unless they are given this soaking before they are arranged. I have been unsuccessful in conditioning young fronds of native maidenhair fern (Adiantum pedatum), but older fronds, so hardened, remain fresh· in arrangement for an astonishing length of time. In general, ferns wilt more rapidly than most foliage. If fronds have drooped before you have given them complete immersion, dip

49 DESIGNED FOR COOLING EFFECT *Pilea, philodendron, nephthytis, and sansevieria are combined to suggest the natural growth of these plant materials. An effect of coolness is achieved with water as an integral part of the composition. It is emphasized by the blue-green lining of the container.*
ARRANGER: MRS. ALDRICH BLOOMQUIST   PHOTOGRAPHER: GOPHER STUDIO

50 "JET PROPULSION" *Interpretive design on an appropriately angular board. Cut palmetto in ascending pattern is intensified through a variety of direction as supporting interest. Note the warm and active variegated pittosporum spotlighting the otherwise all-green arrangement. This is vital in pulling the eye forward to stabilize the strong backward swing of the vertical palmetto. Wavy, shiny, tooth-edged leaves of photinia serrulata, with touches of red, add "action." We are reminded that imagination is seeing ordinary things in new relationships.*
ARRANGER: MRS. JOHN D. FRETWELL   PHOTOGRAPHER: AL ALLEMAN

them in very warm water (bath temperature), and wrap them for about one-half hour in newspaper dampened with cold water—then submerge as usual.

The easiest way to apply this conditioning process is to lay the plant material in a laundry or bath tub. To keep it under water, weight it down with newspaper.

With woody and semi-woody stalks, encourage water intake by scraping off about two inches of the outer surface from the cut end and/or split or hammer the ends to break open the water absorbing fibers. Then condition by keeping the branches or sprays at least two hours in cool water, deep enough to come up high on the stalks, or submerge them completely.

An exception is the rose which takes up water through a thin membrane between the heart and the outer covering. Expose this to the life-giving liquid by cutting slits up the stem that will be under water in the arrangement. Unless you want the thorns to add under water interest in a glass container, slice these off too, thereby laying open more of the water sucking agent.

SPECIAL TREATMENT

Some plants require special treatment before soaking. Soft textured or hairy surfaced leaves respond to steeping just the stem ends for a few seconds in about two inches of boiling hot water. Japanese maple and acanthus leaves hold up extremely well if you give them this treatment.

Plants that exude a milky substance, as the crotons and other members of the Euphorbia family, do better by charring the stem ends with a flame.

TREAT THE ARRANGEMENT

It is believed by some that to rub over the surface of broad leaves with waxed paper helps to conserve moisture and so to add life to an arrangement. Whether or not this is so I cannot say. But the practice has value in heightening the color beauty of its plant material.

A constant supply of fresh clean water goes a long way toward keeping your arrangement in good condition. Except with the bother of siphoning, it is not feasible to change it without disturbing the grouping's design. It is enough to add water as it evaporates in the container. Let this be at room temperature to prevent shock which some plants abhor.

Remove all soft porous leaves that are on stems under the water in the finished arrangement, since their rapid deterioration fouls it and hastens wilting. Put one or two walnut size pieces of charcoal to absorb impurities in the container of a design that will remain "on location" for some time. Charcoal helps only to purify the water; it does not serve to prolong life beyond normal span. For this purpose, use one of the manufactured flower preservers available at the florists.

Occasionally take a long-lasting arrangement to the kitchen sink where you can spray the foliage with water. This removes dust and is quite a tonic to the greens.

7

MECHANICAL AIDS

As do all good workmen, have the best possible equipment. This doesn't mean necessarily the most expensive nor the most complicated. Of chief importance is a control device or "holder" without which the loveliest foliage and the most beautiful container may not make a well designed arrangement. Like leaves and containers, their variety is legion. The market offers hundreds of styles made of lead, steel, brass, wood, plastic. Even so, all may be classified according to a few general types. The following I have found most useful in foliage arrangements.

PINPOINT HOLDERS

First on my list is the pinpoint holder originated in the Orient more than 100 years ago. These have sharp metal pins closely embedded in a heavy base. Plant material is impaled upright on the points, and then pulled into desirable position to remain firmly in place. A leaf with a short petiole or with none at all is held simply by slipping its base end between the pins.

This type is available in various shapes and sizes. It comes in single or interlocking units usable together as a large holder, or in parts as smaller controls. Still others are in cups which hold water. These are ideal used without any other receptacle on a flat base as in Plate 45, or in a container which, like alabaster, doesn't hold water satisfactorily (Plate 39). In time, water causes alabaster to disintegrate; a coating of wax on the inside surface will protect it.

If leaf stems are too fine or too soft to impale on the pins, wedge in bits of thicker stems for support. Or slip them into hollow stalks, as in bamboo or the gladiolus flower stem, and firm this on the holder. Be sure, of course, that water can reach the leaves. Or manage soft stemmed leaves by grouping some together in your hands and reinforcing their stems with florist's thread or fine wire wrapped around them near the base.

Weathered wood can sometimes be anchored by means of a pinpoint holder. If it is too hard or too heavy, mount it on wood blocks or set it in plaster of Paris to give a strong base.

BIRD-CAGE HOLDER

Also for use in a low receptacle, and my favorite for the dining table centerpiece, is the bird-cage type; foliage can be inserted into its wire mesh at various angles. These too come in a variety of shapes and sizes. Some have suction cups to keep them stationary in the bowl.

HOLDER ANCHORAGE

But anchorage is a simple problem in any case. Put three dabs of floral clay at intervals around the base of the holder. Press it down on the bottom of your container with a slight twist. This insures against its slipping. Plasticine (modeling clay) is a poor substitute as it tends to crumble in time.

Another means of anchorage is to pour melted wax or paraffin into the bottom of your bowl where you want the holder, and fit it into this before the substance hardens. When it does, your holder is firmly attached. Fastening in this way is particularly good with silver since some clays tend to oxidize it. If you prefer, a wad of cotton under a holder in silver will render it slip-proof, and will prevent possible surface scratching.

One thing is paramount—the surface of both container and holder must be perfectly dry before the wax or clay is applied.

PLASTIC SUBSTANCE AS CONTROL

For control in a tall vase, nothing surpasses the comparatively new plastic matter. One kind is fluffy bits which are ideal for pouring into a deep, narrow-mouthed vase into which it is difficult to fit a conventional holder. Fill the vase with this porous product to an inch or so of the top, and press down with your fingers until it is tightly packed. Add water to the level of this filler. You can then easily firm plant material in it.

Another sort is a block of expanded plastic that absorbs and holds water. Trim it to fit your container, and soak this in water until fully saturated (it shrinks to about two-thirds of its original size). You can insert branches and heavy stemmed leaves directly into this solid form. For softer stems, first make holes with a sharp instrument. Otherwise they will bend when you apply the pressure needed to insert them.

Being hard fibered, these plastics don't decay as do, in time, fern or privet clippings with which some arrangers stuff their vases for support. When you discard the arrangement, simply remove the plant material, drain off the water, and vase and holder are in readiness for future use; this inexpensive plastic can be used indefinitely.

HOMEMADE DEVICES

But it isn't necessary to rely on standard devices. Homemade controls can be equally effective. Chicken wire cut and then loosely rolled, with rough edges turned in, to fit in the tall opaque vase is practical. For the transparent vase or bowl, cut a piece to extend about one-half inch over the container's opening.

Bend down the extended frame and this simple holder stays in place for easy use. Exercise care, however, that the wire doesn't scratch your container.

Perhaps you would prefer criss-crossing strips of floral tape (used in corsage making) over the container's mouth, leaving openings to accommodate the leaves. The tape is strong enough to support all but the unusually heavy forms.

CARE OF THE HOLDER

A good holder deserves good care. Cleanse it well after each use. Remove bits of materials that are stuck between the pins or in the wire mesh; pipe cleaners come in handy for this. Today the market offers a special tool for straightening pins that have become bent in use. I am familiar with the one known as the "Pin Doctor," obtainable where flower arrangers' supplies are sold.

A LIST OF NEEDS

I suggest that you keep your equipment at a minimum, lest you concentrate on mechanics rather than on design. The following list is suggested as essential for most work:

1. A suitable holder for control.
2. Floral clay for anchorage.
3. Florist's thread or fine gauge wire (#35) to tie delicate stems into bunches for substantial insertion.
4. Wire of heavier gauge (#21) for strengthening and curving leaves (see page 97).
5. Floral or Scotch tape to secure this "ribbing" wire.
6. Plastic water picks (orchid tubes) to accommodate short stems (see page 100).
7. Test tubes or similarly shaped receptacles for use when fresh and dry material is combined (see page 111).
8. Scissors to cut tender stalks.
9. Pruning shears to cut branches.
10. Knife for scraping off bark or splitting branches to encourage water absorption.
11. Hammer or stone to crush stem ends to aid water intake.
12. Glycerine to mix with water for preserving plant material (see page 112).

51 A RHYTHMIC IMPRESSION *The wedge formation of the soup bone accessories is repeated in the angled shape of the driftwood, the dried strelitzia, the verdant philodendron and pothos leaves to produce a harmonious and rhythmic composition. (The dried leaves are secured with tape to the back of the wood). The homemade container is of plumber's lead.*
ARRANGER: EMILY STUEBING   PHOTOGRAPHER: A. F. STUEBING

8

LET'S MAKE THE ARRANGEMENT

If, even with theory well in mind, you are wondering how to apply what you have learned thus far to the actual making of an arrangement, this chapter is for you. It aims to help those who have had little or no practical experience in arrangement activity.

Don't attempt a difficult construction at first. Do simple things using, perhaps, no more than three varieties of leaves.

CONSIDER LOCATION

Your first demand is to visualize the location of your finished arrangement to determine its size and shape. How tall, how wide, how deep must it be to fit comfortably into its space? Is it to be seen from only one side, from various angles in a free-standing plan, or reflected in a mirror? Will it be placed high, low, or at eye level? Decide if it is to be a light airy design or one compact in pattern. Keep in mind that the more complex is the

background, the simpler the arrangement should be. Conversely, the plainer the background, the more complex the design can be.

To come from the general to the specific, let us suppose your problem is to make an arrangement to fit a vertical and rectangular space defined by the architectural limitations of a wall panel. A tall vertical plan would better suit here than a squared or rounded form, for you are aware that in harmony, the eye seeks repetition. Your problem, then, would be to emphasize shape relationship by constructing your arrangement with its top and edges suggesting a rectangular form evident if you were to draw a contour line from one extremity to another.

CHOOSE PLANT MATERIAL

Each leaf has its place in the pattern it helps to produce, and you will select it for a diversity of qualities — the same

52 "FALL WINDS PASSED BY" Lower diagonal spread of branches forward and backward into space is emphasized by placement of the container and top board to direct the eye in the same directions. On a second board of lighter value, force is enough to balance that of high vertical leafy branches.

ARRANGER: MARGUERITE BOZARTH   PHOTOGRAPHER: C. FANDERS

really that you would look for in flowers when designing a floral composition. In general, you will want a combination of so-called body, weight, and transitional foliage.

Among the body types which form the mainstay of your arrangement, curved shapes, as the roundish begonia leaf, the ovid hosta, the palmate lupine, or the deeply cleft peony give you some idea as to the diversity in range. You will use these for emphasis at the center of interest (Plate 34). Sometimes you will select a few color-blotched ones like aucuba, or if a daintier leaf is needed, the variegated ivy, to relieve a monotony of too much of the same green (Plate 44). Or you will use a sculptured leaf form (Plate 46), or deeply ribbed leaves like Hosta to lend texture variation.

Use spiked or straplike leaves, as yucca or clivia, or upswinging curved branches to give height and welcomed variety to the broader body leaves.

Use spray types, like maidenhair fern or vines (one of the ever ready philodendrons, for instance), to develop the silhouette. They give width to your arrangement and serve as transitional material to pull a difference in leaf shapes into rhythmic relationship (Plate 34). These add grace and decorative pattern to the plan by breaking up awkward spaces or straight surfaces, especially at the sides of your plan.

Actually, transitional leaves do the same for your arrangement that shrubs, a transition between low and high growth, do

for your garden picture; they give rhythm to a grouping by directing your eye to various planes in the structure. Because transition is a harmonizer between unlike units and areas, it serves rhythm, and so unity.

If your finished product does not please you, it is almost certain that your pattern asks for transitional material. Use it to build up your skeleton plan, but don't let it confuse it. Maintain the clarity of your linear structure already established by line placements. Be especially cautious if you include airy types as Asparagus plumosus or sprengeri. Too much fine, feathery foliage has an undeterminate quality that is apt to cloud line structure. But use it discreetly, arranging it rather loosely so it fits comfortably into the plan, and it can be a vital, enhancing area rather than a destructive stifling "filler."

Some plants supply foliage usable in any or all categories. An example is the magnolia. This may be cut from the tree and used in long branches for height, in shorter lengths for transition, and separated from the branch for use as body foliage.

ARTIFICIAL CURVING

It is possible to coax a long stiff blade and the too straight branch into adaptable curves. A leaf is curved at the tip or in a spiraled effect (Plate 53), simply by curling it around your index finger and holding it so for a few seconds.

53 HALLWAY DECORATION An old Chinese container holds tri-colored dracaena and mahogany-red plum, to harmonize in size, pattern, and color with a mahogany-and-gold Federal mirror.

ARRANGER: MRS. JOHN M. LANGENBERGER   PHOTO: COMMERCIAL PHOTOGRAPHIC CO., INC.

54 UNCONVENTIONAL DESIGN *Prompted by the emotions, this arrangement gives stimulus in the aggressive angular line of a grape root, bird's nest fern handled to expose the prominent midrib, and angel wing begonia combined in a triangular wood container with black lacquer lining.*
ARRANGER: MRS. ALFRED S. GRUSSNER   PHOTOGRAPHER: A. L. KNOWLTON

Narcissus and tulip leaves are easy to manipulate in this manner. Tansy (Tanacetum crispum) is amenable too. Curl larger leaves, as aspidistra (Plate 22), by rolling them from the tip to the stem end and tying with florist's thread, or fasten with paper clips. After submerging them in water for the required hardening (see page 84), they will retain their curved shapes when the mechanics are removed. Some arrangers manage the very large and heavy leaves by securing a thin wire with floral or Scotch tape along the center rib on the back of the leaf. Curved toward the back, the mechanics won't show.

Apply gentle pressure at the joints of a carnation leaf stalk. Use special care because this stem with its fascinating curlicue foliage tends to snap at these joints.

Woody branches require a little more effort although to curve them with pressure from your hands is not difficult. Hold the branch with your thumbs touching on the underside, and your fingers above where you want the curve. Press down gently with your fingers, and up with your thumbs. At the same time, move them slowly along the stem where the curve is to be. Extremely heavy needled evergreens will respond more readily

55 A TOUCH OF DRAMA *Black-green glossy fern-like cycas repeats the shape, pattern, and basic exterior color of the container; yellow stripes of the rolled dracaena echo the hue of its lining and surface design. Note the value here of handling plant material in an unnatural manner — distortion with a purpose.*
ARRANGER: MRS. RAYMOND RUSS STOLTZ
PHOTOGRAPHER: SEVECKE

if you allow them to wilt slightly first. Then curve, and harden in water. Large stiff cycas leaves are not pliable. (See Plate 55). If these palmlike shapes prove stubborn, tie them to a wire frame (a clothes hanger pulled into circular formation serves well), and then harden in water. In most cases, when you untie the leaves to arrange them, the curved shape remains.

CONSIDER SCALE RELATIONSHIP

Don't overlook the scale relationship of the leaves. To have a rhythmic sequence in size, select an assemblage of large, medium, and small shapes, and group them into areas of like sizes, hues, textures, and line directions. This prevents spottiness prohibitive in organized design. Arrange these in gradation, with leaves decreasing in size from the body of your plan to the surrounding space, and with voids increasing in size. Even the growth of Nature shows graded shapes and lines. Note the sequence in size of leaves on a stalk of hollyhock, or the radial pattern of tree trunk and limbs. Even veining of a leaf illustrates minute directional gradation.

CHOOSE CONTAINER, STAND, ACCESSORY, AND EQUIPMENT

Guided by the preceding chapters, you are ready to decide on your container, your stand if you plan for one, and your accessory if you have reason to include it. Have the well conditioned plant material and the tools of the craft at hand. Make yourself comfortable at your work table and you are ready to begin composition.

WORKING PROCEDURE

Your first step in actual execution is to anchor your control device as explained on page 89. Now fill the container with water. In a one-sided arrangement, begin by placing your tallest line fairly well back in the container to leave room for filling in your design. In a free-standing plan, insert high placement on the middle row of pins thereby allowing room for a well shaped pattern on all sides. Whether this will be at the middle of your plan or just near it will depend on the sort of balance you plan for. If it is to be symmetrical, insert the highest material directly in the center. If an asymmetrical design is your intent, place this to one side of the holder's center.

It is helpful in securing balance if either the tip or the heaviest part of the tallest material is directly over the base or the area from which it rises. Place the rest of your plant material so that it seems to grow easily out of the container and from apparently the same source as does the tallest placement (this, you recall, is the focal point), but don't crowd it all on one plane like a fan. Arrange it to give a three dimensional effect with some space between the forward, backward, and sideway swings (Plate 56). Work from front to back as well as from side to side. Height is determined by the weight low in your design. Except in a

56 VERDANT AND DRIED *Dried prickly fruit of datura and small fresh leaves of cut-leaf philodendron combine admirably in an East Indian container and with the Buddha of the Mountain accessory.*

ARRANGER: MRS. LAMBERT D. LEMAIRE   PHOTOGRAPHER: A. L. KNOWLTON

horizontal pattern, have the tallest material at least one and one-half times the height of the vase or width of the bowl, but it is often more pleasing to have it considerably taller—two times the height or width, or three, perhaps (Plates 58, 59). In a horizontally spread plan, let the swing be as great as pleases your eye but have some short upright lines for the interest that contrast affords (Plate 62). In a pattern which gives dominance to the grace of trailing vines, I find proportions generally pleasing if the vine rises about one-third of the overall height above the container's rim, and hangs two-thirds below. This, of course, is an approximation.

Let spiked and straplike leaves face you, for their beauty is better seen than when their edges face to the front. If you are using daffodil foliage, it is fun to build them together as do the Japanese. When the blades are pulled from the delicate brown sheath that grows around the plant, you will find that each has a sort of pocket at the base. Working in your hand, use these to nestle three or five leaves together. Now cover them with the paperlike sheath, and they are ready to impale on, or insert in, the holder, depending on the sort you are using. Or if you prefer, keep them intact with a bit of florist's thread or fine wire about their stems close to the ends.

FOCUS AREA

To attract attention, let the "eye" of the center of interest face directly forward, but arrange some of the surrounding material at angles as in Plates 19, 57. This goes a long way toward relieving any tightness and flatness in this important area. A swirl of leaves, such as ivy or eucalyptus, does well here.

If the stems of foliage you wish to place low are too short to reach the holder, insert them in water filled orchid tubes. Use those pointed at the end so they are easily held in place between the pins of a pinholder, or in the openings of other controls.

Assure pleasing results in a free-standing arrangement by working against a backbone of foliage (placed on the holder as described above) on one side before turning it around to complete the other. Make the center of interest differ here from that on the other side. This practice will develop pattern that will have more than a momentary interest for the spectator.

The center of interest can accommodate a few flowers you might happen to have on hand. The same pattern of greens can furnish a lasting framework, with the simple substitution of bloom changing the effect from time to time. Plates 62, 67, and 83 exemplify this time-saving device for making a minimum of bloom serve richly in home decoration.

VOIDS ARE IMPORTANT

As you work around and against the structural backbone, pay attention to design-

57 SPACE HAS MEANING *In a white-lined 36-inch oval bowl, variegated foliage is arranged to set off the beauty of ebony-like stems of the black-stemmed Alocasia which complements the lovely sculpture. Harmony through an agreement of spaces and solids—alike in some respects but different in others—is strongly evident.*
ARRANGER: MRS. WILLIAM S. CARPER
PHOTOGRAPHER: STAN SHEETS

ing interestingly shaped voids. It is helpful to use branches or leaves of various lengths thus preventing uniform straightness across the top of your plan. If you are designing with only one hue and tone, plan especially to include plenty of voids. These give an openness of silhouette which does away with the danger of a meaningless blob of color. For every such statement there is always an exception—in this case, Plate 22. Here, responsibility for beauty is given to the perspective gained through the drama of curling and overlapping leaves.

UNIFY CONTAINER AND FOLIAGE

You may wish to unify the hard structure of your container and the more fragile character of the foliage by bringing a leaf or two down over the container's edge. This serves as a transitional area between these unlike parts of your design, but it isn't necessary to completely hide the rim; sometimes exposing some or all of this edge adds interest.

WORK FOR A THREE-DIMENSIONAL EFFECT

It is easier to achieve a "3-D" effect by working from dark areas up to planned highlights. Overlap some of your foliage shapes to lend an illusion of depth. This gives light and shadow to move your eye in and out. Or gain depth by reversing some leaves to show their backs. We learn the value of this from the Japanese artists, but American arrangers are slow in taking full advantage of the skill. Leaves knotted (as you would knot a piece of rope) or looped as in Plate 72 are a help. To gently fold a leaf along its mid-

rib and use it here and there will aid in sculptural effect too (Plate 58). If the leaf is perfectly dry, floral clay at intervals within the fold will maintain it.

Especially in the all green arrangement, these tricks can add drama to make it something quite striking. But such devices are desirable only if you use self-restraint in employing them; overdoing is disastrous. Do not distort for the sole purpose of being different. It is justified only if it has design meaning as the fringed bamboo, Plate 40, the abstracted vein pattern, Plate 82, and the cut leaves, Plates 6 and 63.

It is possible that you will make your own discoveries for distinctive treatment as you construct your arrangement. In visioning it in your mind, you will not anticipate every little detail. Some unusual problem (or possibly some accident!) in making it may challenge you and put your craftsmanship to severe test. You've torn a leaf, perhaps. This is not necessarily a loss. It may be a happy accident which can contribute to an effect of spontaneity always so refreshing. There is nothing wrong with such devices to bring interest to your arrangement providing they are not considered as an end. Like wood pieces, and figurines, and accessories in general, use them sparingly and with purpose.

WORK FOR SIMPLICITY

To attain the worthy goal of simplicity, avoid the natural tendency to use too much plant material. Eliminate any that is not essential to the clarity of your intent.

If you are arranging leafy branches (Plate 53), you will find it advisable to prune out twigs not necessary to your intended design. Cut with a backward slant and darken the wood thus exposed by rubbing over it with a piece of wet bark or a hunk of dampened mud. In this way you render the cut unnoticeable. Many shrubs and trees carry their leaves thickly placed on the branch, and unless these are judiciously pruned, the appearance is of a weighty, dense mass rather than pleasing line. Lilacs and viburnums are notable examples. Plate 76 shows the advantage of pruning to maintain a satisfactorily filled area, but at the same time, to give emphasis to attractive line.

At this point it seems advisable to call to your attention that lack of variety in your plan does not ascertain simplicity —the simple design is one that is unified in all respects. Be sure to decide on a dominant hue, value, texture, shape, and direction of line to set the arrangement's character, but remember that variety which works toward unity can add much interest to your plan. *An arrangement is a simple one when unity is present without being obvious.*

CONCEAL MECHANICS

Conceal unattractive mechanics. A common error in beginners' work is a visible holder not planned as a design element. Hide the part still exposed after you have placed your leaves, by covering it with bark fragments, shells, stones, or an extra leaf or two. Be sure your concealing material is an asset to your design, not obvious in its function. And choose something that suits in character (Plates 58, 49, 57). The beauty of the arrangement can easily be marred. Even the slight appearance of mechanics will destroy the effect.

SELF-CRITICISM

If your first arrangement efforts displease you, don't despair. What is important is the knowledge you have gained, even if results are not to your liking. Only if you fail to improve as you gain in experience, should you feel discouragement.

There follow a few things you can do to check your finished design for faults:

1. Look at it upside-down by facing away from it, bending your body with one hand on your hip, and looking back at your arrangement through the crook of your arm. Or reverse it by looking at its reflection in a mirror. Either way, "realism" is lessened and enables poor balance to be more easily recognized.
2. Look at your arrangement from a distance. This minimizes details to better display its silhouette, interesting or not.
3. Place it in a comparatively dark area to determine poor or effective highlighting.
4. Place it in intense light to better realize a subtle rendition of value variations.

Making a foliage arrangement is somewhat like playing a game of cards. Only after the concluding effect of a played card is considered, does the player make it. And so it is in arranging. Whether your material is of one hue or another, dull or shining, delicate or strong, is not as important as what you do with it. Only by "playing" with your leaves do you come to recognize the final result. Add every leaf with its effect in mind; each tone mass as a shape to direct your eye to all others, and thus bring order rather than spottiness to your grouping. At first you may have to think about the things discussed here, but eventually you will come to feel them as second nature.

You are the lucky one if you work by instinct and so, spontaneously. But if you must concentrate intently as you arrange, don't be concerned. If you grow tired, stop for a while. When you return to your task, you will be rewarded with a freshened eye and stimulated to finishing your plan without making it look "tired and worn." Do not force yourself. The important thing is to arrange with pleasure.

58 ELOQUENT RESTRAINT *A simplicity of design in space divisions made with but five units—two leaves of ginger (one folded for silhouette interest), one spearhead nephthytis, one heart-shaped calla lily, and a chartreuse earthenware container.*
ARRANGER: HANS CHRISTIAN ANDERSON MADISON   PHOTOGRAPHER: JACQUES SAPHIER

9

PERMANENT PRESERVATION

PRESERVE BY DRYING

Foliage cut for drying is not soaked, of course, before you arrange it. Wash it, if you like, but your aim is to handle it so that moisture leaves the leaf tissues as quickly as is possible, leaving brittle beauty that, in many cases, rivals that of the living leaf. In general, cut the leaves to be dried just as they come into maturity.

UPSIDE-DOWN METHOD

Tie the leaves into loose bunches (circulation of air about the leaves prevents molding), and hang upside-down in a dry, warm atmosphere. Allow two weeks for the drying period.

Large linear leaves, like canna or corn, with but few exceptions will dry in this manner with very little curling at the edges. In fact, they will be stiff and straight in most cases. To secure some curves, dry a few over a rounded surface, or coax them into desired shape by running them through your fingers now and then in the early stages of drying. Aspidistra tends to crinkle unattractively, but when it has thoroughly dried, press it with a warm, not hot, iron.

VARIANT METHODS

There are a few exceptions that cure more gracefully if allowed to do so right side up, and gradually in a darkened room, and at a cool temperature. Notable examples are gladiolus leaves, silver-leaved poplar (Populus alba), nasturtium foliage, African silver tree (Leucadendron argenteum), and the artemisia commonly known as "dustymiller." All gray leaves dry nicely, but this variety gives best results if you put the stem ends in just a little water and let the leaves dry gradually. If you cut branches of the alba poplar on a hot summer's day, and dry in this way, you will be amazed at the results. The leaves dry to brown with white linings. When the branches are arranged, they look for all the world as though they were covered with newly fallen snow. The nasturtium, with this method, curls up slightly, but it is unusual in retaining a green hue with a decided yellow at the leaf's center.

I have discovered a few other exceptions to the upside-down process. Large banana leaves dry into beautifully curved shapes on a flat surface. The cucumber magnolia (M. acuminata) takes on lovely curves when "flat dried," as do the leaves of Hosta (Plate 9) and rubber plant (Ficus lyrata). Incidentally, a coating of liquid brown shoe polish emphasizes the leathery texture of the beautiful large shapes of the latter.

All leaves such as you would dry for body weight in your design, tend to curl at the edges. But like the nasturtium, this gives form interest. If you wish some flat, dry them on a hardware cloth platform raised for air circulation. Pebbles at intervals on the leaf edges prevent curling. A leaf with its stem protruding from the under surface, rather than from the base, is placed with this petiole through an opening in the wire mesh. I dry rosettes of common field mullein (Verbascum) this way, flattening the clump with my hand from time to time during the drying period.

Branches cut in their dormant stage dry into curved shapes easily if tied to a wire clothes hanger frame pulled into desired shape. The Scotch broom in Plate 60 was treated so.

PRESS TO RETAIN NATURAL HUE

For the most part, dried leaves are subtle in hues of biege, gray, or brown, but it is possible to include other hues as well in your supply of dried foliage. Croton retains its coloring; ginkgo, maple, and oak

59 RECOGNIZED AS THE HEIGHT OF QUALITY *Cucumber magnolia dried to a rich dark brown lined with beige in a wooden compote.*
ARRANGER AND PHOTOGRAPHER: MRS. ROBERT GODLEY

60 CONTRAST IN TEXTURE *The bulk of silvery-gray driftwood is nicely balanced by a cluster of rich brown glycerinized magnolia leaves and tall curving lines of dark green dried Scotch broom. Grayish light green, naturally dried magnolia gives pleasing transition between the wood and the rough bark base so wisely chosen for this attractive design.*

ARRANGER: MRS. JAMES CASSIDY   PHOTOGRAPHER; MEL MANLEY

leaves hold their height of fall coloring if you dip them in melted paraffin and then iron them between soft paper (newspaper will do). Cluster them into rosette formation for dramatic center of interest material.

I once made a Christmas wreath from the golden fall leaves of the ginkgo tree. I gathered them as they fell, and pressed them as described above. Four hundred were required for the average size garland made on a frame fashioned from a wire clothes hanger. To make such a wreath, prepare the leaves by passing a twelve-inch length of fine wire through each leaf near its base. With six inches on each side, turn the wire down and twist it around the stem. This wire supplies a means of attaching the leaves to the foundation. Place them in groups of three as you would in making the familiar wreath of ivy. For neatness, arrange the groups in succession, with the notched ends of one cluster overlapping the stem ends of the preceding one to conceal the mechanics. To give finesse, thicken the completely covered frame at what will be the bottom when it hangs. I trimmed mine with small green blown-glass tree balls to echo the hint of green edging on the leaves; you will think of other possibilities. You can assemble such a wreath at your leisure early in the season, or if you prefer, prepare the leaves and fashion them into a wreath nearer the Christmas holiday.

The lovely white-veined silverleaf fittonia (F. argyroneura) is a special joy when pressed between the paper sheets *without* waxing. Sumac and ferns too, press in this way and hold their shapes as well as hues. The lack of light preserves color to match the natural hue.

If you enjoy experimenting, take a few fern fronds and pinnately-compounded sumac leaves from the improvised presser before they have thoroughly dried. Let them finish the drying process on a flat surface, or upright in a jar (without water). Sometimes, their structures take on attractive curves.

If you have room for large folds of newspaper spread on the floor, you can press whole branches of tree leaves in the manner of the eighteenth century homemakers. Cut branches while the leaves are still green, or just as they are beginning to turn in the autumn, or after they have taken on their most vivid hues. The important thing is that the branches are still full of sap—otherwise, leaves will shatter when dry. Prune the twigs so the branches lie as flat as is possible, and trim them so there is no overlapping of leaves. Dry as many layers of branches at one time as you wish, using paper between each and on top. Weight the branches down with flat boards. Place something heavy on this to keep them compressed. After about three weeks, the branches are ready for arranging. So handled, the leaves retain their natural hue, but the branches are undeniably flat. We are told by those responsible for drying material this way for winter decoration in the buildings of "Restored Williamsburg" that oak, dogwood, maple, hickorynut, and beech give the best results.

One can dry plant material in borax to retain natural shape and color. While this process is excellent for drying flowers, I do not find it of any advantage with foliage.

TIPS ON USING DRIED LEAVES

To show off the lovely dried forms, choose a container of simple shape, dull

61 WITH AN ORIENTAL AIR *On a slab of manzanita the purplish-mottled pale green stems of Jack-in-the-pulpit's new growth give unusual interest. Light green chickweed brings the "scale" down to the Chinese figure in green and brown.*
ARRANGER: FLORENCE M. SCHAFFER   PHOTOGRAPHER: MEL MANLEY

finish, and subtle hue. If you use a vase, fill it with sand or one of the plastic fillers; dried stems are easily inserted in either. In a low receptacle, use any workable holder (see page 88). Since dried material is brittle and so subject to breakage, pour melted wax or paraffin over the top of the holder after the design is completed. With this added protection the arrangement will last without mishap as long as you want it.

For added height, attach wire "stems" to leaves. This also makes possible a flexibility denied the leaves themselves, and lends more freedom in designing. You may reshape your dried material, should you desire to do so. First soften it by soaking it one-half hour in water. Then mold it as described on page 97.

Don't hesitate to combine dried material with fresh as in Plate 56, for you will agree that Nature reveals no definite division between life and death—the end is a beginning, not a complete stopping. For the sake of dominance, the character principle, have one or the other, fresh or dried, predominate. Let the other play a subordinate role in your design. Dried branches, even budded or leafed, aren't harmed in water, but if left in too long, dried foliage is. To keep the latter dry, insert the ends in empty orchid tubes. If they are too large for these small vials, use any narrow bottle with a suitable opening. Chemical test tubes are ideal; any similar shape in glass or plastic will do.

STORE WITH CARE

It is fun to dry various leaves as they come into maturity and lay them away for future use. Like the tucked away

Christmas tree ornaments, each time the box is opened, its contents will evoke happy response. But store them in a dry place as they mold in slightest dampness. Most dried material keeps indefinitely, but there are exceptions. Aspidistra, gladiolus, iris, and sansevieria dry well and will last for many weeks, but their attractiveness is not permanent.

The dried leaves shown in these illustrations and mentioned in this text are not exhaustive in possibility, surely, but perhaps enough to challenge you to try for your own discoveries.

PRESERVE WITH GLYCERINE

From France has come knowledge of the glycerine method of preserving shrub and tree branches. First, cleanse the leaves by

62 FOR THE ARRANGER'S DESK *Jack pine (Pinus banksiana) with Christopher Stone red roses arranged in dark green heavy glass book ends.*
ARRANGER: MRS. JOE E. WOLFF   PHOTOGRAPHER: ROBERT D. PETERSON

washing them well in sudsy water. Rinse well. Then place branch ends that have been split and scraped to encourage absorption, in about a three-inch deep solution of one-third glycerine and two-thirds water. Wipe each leaf with a soft cloth dampened with this liquid to help prevent leaf drying before glycerine saturation takes place. Circulation of air about the leaves is helpful, so don't crowd the branches in the receptacle. As the water evaporates, replenish it, but no more glycerine will be required.

COLOR AND TEXTURE

Glycerine treated branches are pliable, and the leaves are silken in texture. The eventual change in color varies with the plant, the time of gathering, and the length of time in the solution. Most leaves turn bronzy in tone although there are exceptions. The naturally bronzy-red and bronzy-purple leaves retain their original hue and texture after curing. If treated in the spring, barberry turns to a bright red; in autumn, to brown. Beech will be brown if it is preserved in the spring and tan if in the fall. The lovely lobed foliage of hawthorn turns to a dark rose. Aucuba is unique in its color change to a very glossy brownish-black.

Laurel, rhododendron, loquat, magnolia, and rosettes of pittosporum take the glycerine nicely. In fact, almost any leaf of strong substance is satisfactory. Thin-textured materials, like plum and crabapple, generally begin to droop if they are in the solution longer than one week; remove them at the first sign of wilt. They remain their normal hue and their lasting quality is satisfactory. Rough leaves, as a rule, can't be preserved with glycerine, although the wrinkled foliage of leatherleaf viburnum (V. rhytidophyllum) does well for me—it remains rough in texture, is green or brown depending on how long it is in the solution.

TIME REQUIRED

For complete absorption, a two week period is required by most branches. Some, however, need a longer time if you want the change in color to spread to the edges of the leaves. This designates that they have had their fill, and when they are removed from the solution, will remain indefinitely as they are.

After about one-half the time required for saturation, some leaves, like the viburnum mentioned above, are still green. Others are partly their natural hue and partly changed in color. Elaeagnus leaves, for example, are still dominantly green, just hinting at the bright burnished yellow to which they will turn after four weeks in the solution. Even at this stage, the leaves keep well.

PRESERVING INDIVIDUAL LEAVES

When the stem ends of long linear leaves, as iris, dracaena, canna, and aspidistra, are soaked in the liquid, they tend to dry at the tips before the glycerine can reach here. No amount of surface application seems to prevent it. But it is a simple matter to cut these to characteristic shape, removing the dried portion in the process.

63 VERTICAL YUCCA, cut back, reveal strong upthrust of cattails. Clinkers conceal the holder.
ARRANGER: RAE L. GOLDSON
PHOTOGRAPHER: BRAMORE STUDIO

You may prefer the complete coverage method for glycerine curing of individual leaves. For plants that grow close to the ground absorbing moisture through their leaves, this means is a must. Mix *equal* parts of water and glycerine and stir well. Completely immerse the leaves in this until their tissues have assimilated the glycerine. Foliage of soft substance, as the grape, does not preserve satisfactorily. But tough varieties, as ivy and lily of the valley, take readily to the bath, and you can use them in arrangement many times over.

Pandanus and sansevieria will not respond to glycerine with any degree of success, but these leaves will last a long time without water and untreated.

COLOR WITH DYE

Do you admire the black magnolia and the bronzy, deep red oak leaves most florists keep on hand? If you are ambitious and are extremely careful to protect your hands and clothing from the "treating bath," you can produce these yourself. Leaves of hard substance can be so preserved and dyed—laurel and palm have been especially interesting to me.

Make "Javelle Water" by dissolving four pounds of washing soda to a gallon of water. Add a pound of chloride of lime. Mix and store this in a wooden receptacle or stone crock as this liquid corrodes metal. Dilute the solution with one-half water for all leaves except oak. Because of the large quantity of tannin in these, the solution is diluted only one-fourth. After soaking the leaves until they are bleached (from twelve to thirty-six hours), remove them from the bath and rinse them thoroughly in water. Now put them in cotton fabric dye of any hue, fol-

lowing directions on the package. If you want them black, soak them in liquid black shoe polish. After they have achieved the desired color, rinse them carefully. Make them pliable by submersion in a five percent solution of glycerine after which dry them for use over an indefinite period of time.

Commercially, branches as well as individual leaves are so treated, but the large receptacle they demand is not available to the average arranger.

USE AND CARE OF TREATED FOLIAGE

Unlike dried foliage, the glycerine treated is not damaged by water, so don't hesitate to combine fresh and treated leaves or branches in a design. If dust collects on the surface of treated material, restore it to beauty by washing or wipe over the leaves with a wet cloth.

And like dried foliage, it can be stored in boxes between periods of use. The glycerine solution too can be used over and over. Save it in a sealed jar.

PRESERVE THROUGH SKELETONIZING

And at the florist you can purchase "angel wings" or "shadow leaves" (Plate 64). These are avocado or magnolia foliage treated to reveal their intricate lacelike pattern of veins and nerves after the fleshy part has been removed. These skeletonized leaves are gossamer-sheer and ethereal looking either bleached to whiteness, or dyed to pale hues, but they wear superbly and are quite sturdy.

It is not uncommon in the winter months to find naturally skeletonized foliage on the ground—leaves from which all

64 AN IMPRESSIONISTIC IDEA *To express "Atomic Explosion," an overlay of cream colored, skeletonized leaves fluff out in a full design, and grade down to golden and deep brown magnolia, naturally dried. Dried heads of yarrow pull the whole together, while twisted stems of dried garlic add to the theme. These and a few of the background leaves are sprayed with gold to pick up the touches of brass on the television for which this arrangement was planned as decoration. The container is mahogany.*

ARRANGER: MRS. ROBERT E. CREIGHTON   PHOTOGRAPHER: ARCHIE BIBBEY

living substance has gone, leaving the structure intact.

CURE YOUR OWN

But it is a challenge to prepare your own as did the homemakers of the Victorian era. Their method was a rather long and messy process; a comparatively simple one is as follows:

Soak any hard textured leaf in a bath prepared by adding two tablespoons of ordinary household bleach (I use Clorox) to one quart of water. Ivy, oak, maple, laurel, magnolia, and holly are especially beautiful. Select leaves without blemishes as such imperfections will be unattractive thick areas on the skeletonized leaf. After at least an hour's soaking (a little longer is sometimes required), transfer the foliage to a rinse of clear water. Now with a soft cloth, gently wipe away any soft fleshy part that still remains. Put the leaves between paper toweling and press in a magazine. After twenty-four hours, these misty looking leaves are ready for use. Curve them by curling them around your finger.

One ingenious arranger made "lilies" from skeletonized sea grape, a shrublike tree (Coccolobis), that grows abundantly in Florida. She rolled and wired them to resemble a calla lily in shape, and with brown floral tape, wrapped the stem to cover the mechanics.

PRESERVE WITH PAINT OR VARNISH

And still another means of preservation is to brush leaves with clear white varnish, the same that artists use as a fixative on paintings. This treatment renders hard surfaced leaves, like dracaena or rubber plant (Ficus), decoratively glossy; their long lasting beauty is quite effective. A varnish coating prevents rhododendron and ivy foliage from curling when they are used without water as they often are in Christmas decoration.

Several coats of enamel paint preserves leaves and gives a finish to simulate porcelain, should such fit into your decorative scheme. If you wash foliage before applying an artificial finish, be sure the water has thoroughly dried. Moisture prevents an even coating.

65   FREE-STANDING ASYMMETRICAL BALANCE   *Green zamia foliage (Coontie) with its rust-red seed pods (male and female) in an antique bronze container.*
ARRANGER: ZELDA WYATT SCHULKE   PHOTOGRAPHER: JACKSONVILLE, FLORIDA NEWSPAPER

10

FORCING FOR UNUSUAL BEAUTY

One of the thrills that comes with arrangement is the awareness of the beauty in dormant branches. They hint of life in repose—just waiting for the warmth of spring sun to unfold their buds with the message of renewed life. They are a special joy in late winter arrangements.

CUTTING AND PREPARING

Cut branches on any mild day; freezing weather hinders success. The time required to force slumbering buds into the delicacy of indoor leaves depends on when they are cut. The nearer this is to the normal development, the less time is required. But you can begin forcing with the coming of the new calendar year.

Select branches at least twenty-four inches in length and about finger thickness, for there must be enough sap for growth activity; short twigs do not contain sufficient life-giving substance. You can shorten branches to various lengths when you are ready to arrange them. Remember to cut on a slant away from you, at a node to prevent blunt stubby tips, and conceal the cut as explained in Chapter 8.

Prepare the branches for water absorption (see page 87). Now stimulate growth by softening the bark and buds by floating the branches in lukewarm water. As it cools, mold them into desired curves. When you are satisfied with their contour, put their ends in cold water and set them in a cool place for three or four days. Now they can be brought into room temperature and arranged to await the marvel of unfolding life. Warm temperature hastens forcing but produces weak and sickly growth. Just as the drying of leaves should be done quickly, forcing should be done with deliberate slowness.

Experiments have shown that adding commercial preservers to the water

66   A NOTE OF SPRING   *Budded larch branches and daffodil blades in a Japanese O-Gencho* *bronze container. A piece of bark gives unity. Three white daffodils add highlight and are the change-* *able material in this basic pattern.*

ARRANGER: MRS. LAMBERT D. LEMAIRE   PHOTOGRAPHER: A. L. KNOWLTON

67 BASIC PATTERN WITH HOME GROWN MATERIAL *In an alabaster compote and under the influence of line and form, every detail is related and contributes to the whole. Of special note are the radiating patterns of the white veins in the velvety Anthurium crystallinum placed to call attention to their repetition in the amaryllis bloom. Aspidistra leaves give height with the tallest in silhouette to attractively fill the space without being too obvious.*

ARRANGER: MRS. R. C. HART   PHOTOGRAPHER: GEORGE HULL

strengthens the color of leafage, and may open the buds earlier, but I think that the delicacy of coloring in leaves forced without them has a unique and special charm. For me the tests have not assured the advisability of using chemical stimulants.

HINTS ON USING

Arrange the branches alone as in Plate 17, or with other plant material to foreshadow spring in home adornment (Plate 45). The pale green of naturally forced leafage is synonymous with early spring. I like to combine the branches with young weeds, especially dandelions, dug up by the roots. When the soil is washed away, these baby plants last a long time with their roots in water. Try such a plan by arranging low sweeping budded branches at one side of a shallow oval or rectangular bowl. Group tiny green plants at their base with a bit of rock to round out a naturalistic picture inspired by the weeping willow at the edge of a creek, reaching down its branches to the water.

Or choose beautifully shaped branches and arrange them alone for use where they will catch the rays from a nearby lamp. Evenings are still long and the delicate green of the forced leaves is especially effective under artificial light.

CHOOSE WITH THOUGHT

Choose branches for color and growth pattern. Not all are brown and stiff. Among a wide selection you can find swishes of green in broom and Kerria japonica, delightful curves in gray wistaria, interesting formations in red and yellow osier dogwoods (cornus), pendulus wands in yellowish weeping willow. Silver maple

(Acer saccharinum) is a special delight with scaly bark on gray branches. Terminal twigs gracefully droop but curve upward at their tips. This tree flowers first which is worth while, but the deeply cleft and silvery leaves that follow are the special beauty. The red maple (A. rubrum) flowers first too, then develops lovely three-lobed whitish leaves. Its light gray, smooth-barked branches are straight, the terminal twigs quite red. Its buds are small but arranged in clusters which have a richness of detail.

Leaf buds are interesting. Choose branches with an eye to their decorative forms (Plate 66). Plump and conspicuous buds on the unique branch formation of the ginkgo should attract your attention. Hickory (Carya alba) has interesting light golden-brown velvety buds, while those of beech are darker, long, pointed, and smooth. Beech unfolds into small silky, accordion-pleated leaves; dark brown sticky buds of the horse chestnut, into five or seven leaflets hanging downward about the coarse twigs; white oak (Quercus alba), into tiny and fuzzy leaves. And still another character is seen in the deciduous cone-bearing larch. On its gray twigs soft green needles emerge from tiny barrel-like protrusions.

Scars left where old leaves have fallen from the branch add interest. These are horseshoe-shaped and quite showy on sumac and ailanthus. Both spread shiny green leaves feather fashion into the light at the twig ends, and appear to be some exotic material.

It would be senseless to enumerate any more branches that are amenable to this "winter gardening" practice of forcing. Much of your pleasure will come through your own observations.

11

ARRANGEMENTS IN GLASS

Transparent containers are more difficult to handle than those that are opaque, since the stems and, for that matter, the water, become an important part of the whole. Plan for plenty of interesting voids in the design's pattern. This gives a feeling of lightness and of space that is apparent in the glass itself.

The more delicate the glass, the daintier are the leaves that look well arranged in it. Heavy glass can accommodate the heavier material. Some is translucent rather than transparent, and under water design is little more than suggested to the eye; these containers do not require as much skill in handling as do those which are transparent.

In either case, be sure to have the water line either very low in the container (just enough water to cover the stem ends), or very high (up to the rim), to prevent a water line from dividing the vase area into displeasing proportions. The whole problem is really one of balance—the area

below the container's rim must have enough attraction for the eye to compensate for that above. Stems must be long enough to reach to the bottom of the container, or at least appear to be, for stability. You can employ separate stems to approximate the effect, but conceal the union of under and above water designs. Foliage brought down over the rim, outside or inside, will do the trick for you.

A leaf anchored low under the water will add weight if needed and can often be used to fill the gap between the bottom of the vase and the ends of stems not long enough to reach here. Keep the underwater material together (you may have to tie it) so that it seems to rise from a single source as you would in any composition. In the arrangement in glass, the design begins at the very bottom of the container.

Use only leaves of hard substance under water; those of a soft, porous variety, as the hollyhock or the grape leaf, be-

68 TO HONOR ST. FRANCIS OF ASSISI *Arranged in a twenty-one-inch plow disc painted a flat black are five branches of nandina with much of the foliage removed—an appropriate setting for a two-foot statue of the wandering minstrel, hand-carved of Portuguese stone.*
ARRANGER: FLORENCE M. SCHAFFER   PHOTOGRAPHER: MEL MANLEY

come water logged and unattractive within a very short time.

MECHANICS

To anchor the plant material to the bottom, use lumps of glass if available to you, or ordinary clear glass marbles, even pebbles will do. In a narrow-necked vase in which placement would be difficult, impale the stems and leaves on a small pinpoint holder and drop the whole to the bottom of the vase. Conceal the holder with a leaf, the blade of which falls over its short stem in the holder.

UNDER A GLASS-TOPPED TABLE

Do you have a coffee table, or a desk, perhaps, protected by a glass top? If so, a novel and beautiful effect is yours if you make a design with leaves under the glass.

Select hard textured, flat leaves and harden them as usual. Remove the glass and place the well dried foliage in an interesting pattern at the corners of the wooden surface. Or design a garland of leaves to follow the contour of your furniture. When the glass is in place, the leaves keep their green freshness for ten days or more, and the result is striking.

THE BELL GLASS ARRANGEMENT

For a novel idea, clip a few leaves from your window garden and arrange these in a water-filled cup pin holder. Slip a glass dome (cloché) over them and you'll be amazed at the show-case glamour the surrounding glass imparts to the simple grouping.

Select foliage in scale with the dome. Leaves must be small enough to allow

ample space around them. To avoid confusion, use only two or three varieties at the most.

Should the glass "fog" from condensation, insert small wedges of cardboard or a few match sticks under the dome's rim to let in a little air of room temperature.

This style is a contemporary adaptation of the Victorian conventional arrangements of artificial or waxed flowers under domes, and so is appropriate not only in the strictly modern home, but in the traditional setting as well.

VARIATIONS ON A THEME

For a vertical pattern, arrange tall greens and place a hurricane lamp glass over the grouping. Keep the leaves narrow in design to prevent crowding against the sides of the glass. A pair of these arrangements on your mantel, sideboard, or dining table will give an effect of cool elegance on the hottest summer day.

As another variation of the Victorian style, stage an arrangement of leaves entirely below the rim of a wide mouthed, transparent glass container with water as low as is possible and still cover the stem ends. Let its design follow the contour of the glass, but allow space between the sides of the container and the foliage to prevent a crowded look. You will be pleased with proportions if the highest placement comes to just below the container's opening. Again, emphasis is on coolness.

THE BUBBLE BOWL

The bubble bowl known as the "aquatic arrangement" is a revival of an old art. A rounded vessel is completely filled with water, the opening at the bottom. A spe-

31 GUIDED BY AN ALERT EYE *This work, the result of an eye that sees the influence of one thing on another, is best explained in the words of the arranger: "Florist's ferns 'gone by' carry out the mood established by the gaunt bronze dog. Peperomia strengthens the base line."*
ARRANGER: MRS. LAMBERT D. LEMAIRE   PHOTOGRAPHER: A. L. KNOWLTON

70 LEFT EXCLUSIVELY STYLED
Like a relic of an ancient tree, a weathered and majestic spire of dunwood rises in fitting stateliness behind an antique figure of a Franciscan monk on a teakwood scroll. Counter-interest in green castor bean leaves gives a pleasant contrast to the gray of their undersides and harmonizes with the predominantly gray and brown composition.
ARRANGER: ZELDA WYATT SCHULKE

71 RIGHT CABBAGES AND QUEENS *is an appropriate title suggested by the arranger. Subtle blending of creamy yellow to delicate yellow-green coupled with the almost translucent quality of the cabbage and the white jade figurine have produced a composition exquisite in texture and color.*
ARRANGER: MRS. W. HARRELL WILSON
PHOTOGRAPHER: MILLS STEELE

cially constructed receptacle can be purchased, but it isn't difficult to substitute your own. Use any clear glass receptacle provided its mouth will fit tightly on a base of soup plate shape. Choose one of rounded contour if you want the foliage beautifully magnified (this is so with any plant material under water). Watch the scale of the leaves you select, keep the arrangement low, and give it ample space.

The simplest method of working is to arrange the leaves in your hand, and wrap the base of the stems together with a narrow strip of sheet lead; include a short stemmed leaf to fall over the lead for concealment. The weight of the strip serves as a sinker and steadies the grouping, keeping it from bobbing about. This leaf also gives an appearance of stability.

Stand the assembled foliage upright on the dish and submerge it to the bottom of a large receptacle previously filled with water. Be sure it is large enough to permit the entire proceedings to be done under water; the laundry tub is useful. Now submerge the glass bowl until no air remains in it, and bring it over the arrangement. Fit it down securely on the dish. Bring

72 TIED WITH A BOW-KNOT OF LEAVES *On a beautiful teakwood stand, dracaena leaves are pleasantly coupled with a heavy candle which matches exactly the rose edging on the dark green foliage.*

ARRANGER: MRS. MERRITT ENGLAND   PHOTOGRAPHER: C. G. BARNELL

the whole to the surface, allowing water to remain around the bowl's rim to tightly seal the ensemble and prevent its emptying.

Place the arrangement where it will be undisturbed; in a short time tiny bubbles will begin to form on the edges of the leaves. After about twelve hours, the outline of each leaf appears to be attractively framed with silvery beads.

Bubble bowl arrangements are especially affective where light shines through. Keep them out of direct sun, however, if you wish to enjoy their beauty for a reasonably long time.

Arrangements in glass require the expert touch, but they are well worth the extra effort and thought that goes into them. Glass provides a lucidity and luster which adds sparkle to the quietest corner.

12

THE EVERGREENS IN

CHRISTMAS ARRANGEMENT

THE USE OF CONIFERS

In the winter garden, evergreens take on importance since they do not have to compete with deciduous plants. Even so, it was not until the need of conservation brought protection to the traditional holly of the wild, that needled evergreens became an indispensable material to the holiday arranger. Today we can purchase commercially grown holly, but greens from the coniferous shrubs and trees in the garden top the list in popularity.

Of all Christmas decorations the crèche is the most cherished. Symbolic of the rustic setting of the Christ Child's birth, woodsy needled evergreens seem a particularly fitting background for the familiar figures. To keep the picture natural, arrange them without an ornamental receptacle, on a rough hewn plank, on a strip of bark, or on a flat stone. Use a water-filled pinpoint cup holder to support and keep them fresh. A water-saturated piece of the recently introduced plastic block (see page 89) will do for a holder, or even a white potato. The latter contains enough moisture to maintain freshness in the greens, and due to its earthy hue, is easily concealed. Simply push the branches into its flesh.

Used as a skeleton foundation, the charm of needled evergreens depends on the beauty of line for effectiveness. Use only a few branches; one is often enough. More than three is apt to hide linear structure.

You can search out naturally curved sprays, but this material is easy to curve (see page 97). Keeping the importance of line in mind, prune away foliage that is too thick. Remember that in so doing, an area will be adequately filled without being bulky and lineless.

73 DESIGNED TO BE LOOKED DOWN UPON *Cycas and chicken wire bells with cones are gilded to match a pair of golden doves used at the opposite end of a large coffee table.*
ARRANGER AND PHOTOGRAPHER: MRS. WALTER M. BASCH

COLOR OF THE CONIFERS

Color in coniferous foliage varies from the bright green plumes of Sawara cypress to the rich, dark green of yew (Taxus). Silvery needles of the white spruce (Picea glauca) are particularly decorative though their stiffness is more difficult to use than the irregular growth of the grayish Jack pine (Pinus banksiana). Some of the spruces and cedars boast of steel-blue foliage. The Japanese umbrella pine (Sciadopitys) with its three- to five-inch long, glossy, dark green needles in whorls about its twigs, has a magnificence of dignity.

Perhaps the most graceful of our North American conifers is the hemlock (Tsuga canadensis). Its flattened tiers of short, fine textured, deep green needles with whitish bands on the undersides work up beautifully when you want a graceful and airy line. In overheated rooms its needles

fall quickly, but I have discovered that a teaspoon of a completely balanced plant food to each quart of water in the container will discourage dropping to a marked degree.

Such nutrients in the water sometimes continue growth. I once had yew (Taxus) root in this practice, and in the spring I planted it outside where it has flourished now for seven years.

For all around versatility, I like nothing better than the gray-green juniper. This is easy to shape and pruning of its prickly needles is easily concealed among its dense foliage. Quite in contrast to the unfriendly pricks of this green is the lovely fir—soft as a kitten's fur.

These are only a few of the impressive conifers. In the family of pines alone there are more than sixty varieties growing throughout the United States. Pine, incidentally, holds particular sentiment for New Englanders. The soft hue of the statuesque tree was the only green the Pilgrims saw when they landed in the New World.

BROAD LEAVES FOR CONTRAST

To contrast the needled conifers, look to the broad-leaved evergreens. A single cluster of rhododendron, laurel, or Japanese azalea from your garden shrubs, or a rosette of the ground cover, Japanese spurge (Pachysandra terminalis), is good for center of interest emphasis with the taller greens. Native oak is combined with Jack pine in Plate 79.

Don't overlook "The Holly and The Ivy" in Christmas decoration. With their ancient symbolism of wisdom and friendship, these leaves are as much a part of tradition as is this old French song. And the "Golden Bough" of mistletoe is a part of our Christmas customs. Its strong contrast to the tree on which it chooses to grow as a parasite is no doubt responsible for the magic with which the ancient Druids endowed it. Today we understand that there is no mystery in its unusual growth habit, but a sprig of the yellow twig with pale green leathery leaves and interesting berries is indissolubly associated with Christmas festivities.

Many of the broad-leaved evergreens, especially the small or fine leaved types, are good for line structure as well. In a low bronze container, the arching leucothoe (L. catesbaei) in its bronzy-red winter hue combined with an emphasis of English ivy in its winter garb is a thing of beauty for many weeks.

If you plan to use holly from your own tree, I suggest that you cut the sprays you will need before hard frost overtakes your garden. Keep them in a cold place with their scraped and split branches in water. This insures a brighter green than they will be if you wait until Christmas time to cut them.

DRAMATIC TOUCHES

To simulate the snow on outdoor winter shrubs and trees by covering your cut

74 IN CANDLELIGHT *A sequinned and glitter-dusted pink glass holder and gilded fruits express a joyous mood.*
ARRANGER: MRS. F. PALMER HART   PHOTOGRAPHER: WILLIAM SEVECKE

75 LEFT **TIMELESS IN APPEAL** *This composition of long-needled pine whitened and arranged in bulk to follow the line of candles, shares honor with Plates 73 and 74 for an expression of joy. Blown-glass tree balls, here and there, add sparkle in candlelight reflection. The steps are of styrofoam.* ARRANGER: MRS. FRED MULTALER   PHOTOGRAPHER: MINNEAPOLIS STAR

76 RIGHT **RICH IN SPIRITUAL CONNOTATION** *Thickly-leaved evergreen azalea is pruned to reveal its beauty of line and thereby better relate it in spirit and design to the lovely Madonna and Child, a ceramic copy of an old Italian sculpture, and to the high stand. The elevation renders appropriate dignity to the figure and foliage branches.*
ARRANGER: MRS. RAYMOND P. WISMER   PHOTOGRAPHER: CLASSIC STUDIO

greens with artificial snow is logical, and often very beautiful (Plate 77). As compared to older methods, today's process is easy. Simply follow the directions on a tin of "snow." It is obtainable in white or pale hues at hardware stores during the pre-Christmas season. A press of your finger sprays a delicate and effective coating on your arrangement. Southern live oak (Quercus virginiana) sprinkled fairly heavily with the white resembles the beautiful small-leaved whitish desert holly (Chenopodium) which is today protected by law.

For a gala treatment, dress your greens with gold, silver, or enameled paint (Plate 73). The step from natural greens to the brightening with paint or with artificial materials as plastic stars or tree balls (Plate 75) hung on branches, is natural since the quiet tones of evergreens are all the more subdued when seen in the comparatively dim light of December. Silvered or gilded leaves, or foliage coated with bright enamel paint, tree balls, plastic snowballs, and the like, are also attractive as center of interest material in a grouping of evergreens at Christmas time.

When artificial color is applied to greens, use restraint. I think you will enjoy them more if you brush the paint over them ever so lightly so that their natural hue shows through. Another favored treatment is to touch the leaf with color just toward the edges and while still wet, sprinkle it with "glitter dust" purchased wherever decorative materials are sold.

It has become a custom in many homes to stage an arrangement of greens before a tray that stands upright against a wall. In such a setting the "pruned for line"

beauty of the foliage is seen at its best— in contrast, and in added drama.

Writing of backgrounds brings to mind the possibility of using large leaves, natural or painted, behind a cherished Christmas accessory. For unusual beauty, place an ivory colored madonna figurine before a gilded palmetto. If your figure is too small to be in pleasing scale relationship, raise it on a series of bases in step formation until the height pleases you. The leaf looks like a many pointed star and is reminiscent of that which led the Wise Men on that wonderful night so long ago. Or for simple dignity, stand a white pottery madonna before a single green leaf of a calla lily; upright on its stalk, it gives in effect, a Gothic arch. A large leaf so used will hold its shape and remains attractive for a week or more without water if you completely coat the back with varnish or clear shellac.

Leaves so treated, as ivy or rhododendron, can be used in wreath making— they will not curl as they dry out.

CANDLE FLAME AT CHRISTMAS

Candle flame provides drama in casting shadow patterns over Christmas decorations, especially if they are arranged in front of a lustrous surface, a polished tray or mirror, perhaps. And candles lend symbolism too, so appreciated at Christmas.

Just as you are careful of the scale in a figure you use with an arrangement, be so in your selection of candles. The large heavy one is as wisely chosen for use with the large leaves in Plate 72 as are the less weighty hand-dipped tapers combined with the more delicate greens in Plate 75.

78 ABOVE ESPALIER TREE FOR CHRISTMAS In a sand-filled gilded carton cones and artificial fruits against a silhouette of leaves are attached to a frame shaped from wire hangers.
ARRANGER: MRS. H. RENWIC PEET   PHOTOGRAPHER: CHARLES S. EATON

79 CHRISTMAS IN WASHINGTON *To follow circular pattern of the platter, Jack pine (Pinus banksiana) from high in the Cascades, yellow to reddish-brown oak from the Goldendale area, sumac fruit from the central region, with native moss and musical monks, are designed for a recreation room.*

ARRANGER: MRS. JOE E. WOLFF   PHOTOGRAPHER: ROBERT PETERSON

13

MODERN ARRANGEMENT

Art expression is an evolving creative experience, always undergoing a succession of changes. Although it is difficult to categorize the art of one's own time, flower arrangements today are often described as *contemporary modern* and *modern abstract*. These terms signify new ways of treating and combining plant material—ways relevant to contemporary concepts.

DESIGN IS PARAMOUNT

Modern artists have rediscovered the importance of design and are placing increasing stress on it. In architecture, for instance, building materials such as wood, concrete, aluminum, and steel are appreciated for their own sake and are used in a way that shows their intrinsic characters to advantage.

This book instructs in traditional arranging, for one must become proficient in this more easily executed work before he can hope to be successful with the more difficult modern techniques. Nevertheless, a number of the illustrations, while still associated with the conventional method of assembling, signal a change in attitude toward our floral medium. For example, the arrangements of Plates 18, 80, and 83 are indicative of the modern tendency to show structural elements to best and fullest advantage. With omission of details and nonessentials, the dominant character of the medium becomes more forceful.

DISTORTION FOR DESIGN MEANING

Today's painting and sculpting artists endeavor to heighten the dramatic appeal in their work. In arrangement, this trait finds its counterpart in the distortion of plant material. Such distortion is illustrated (Plate 82) in the new image the arranger has created by removing the flesh from the leaf of a castor-oil plant. Distortion here, in the cut-back foliage in Plates 6 and 63 and in the deeply curved cycas in Plate 55, is not done just for shock value, but for meaningful design. The plant materials are handled in an abstract manner—that is, as symbols of design and not of nature.

SPACE HAS PURPOSE

Because it is space that sets off these created shapes and forms, it takes on greater importance in creation of the design. Note its contribution in the modern-traditional work in Plates 25 and 81. The materials we employ as a medium suggest not only new images to the creative mind, but also new location in the arrangement.

An entirely new concept of *focus* is developing. Emphasis is on the *whole work* rather than centered in a main interest area such as dominates traditional arrangement. For the modern arranger, design becomes free from conformity to set formulae; each arranger can create his own solution to composition, a logical step toward a fuller means of self-expression.

With elements released from a single tyranny of emphasis, spatial areas become an equivalent of solid areas in a new technique of assembling. In fact, it can be said that the truly modern arranger is a designer of space. For the sake of comparison with traditional organization, examine Plates 84 and 85. Note that the plant materials benefit from an individual existence in space and yet are so interrelated that a oneness of space-form structure results from their organization. Emphasis (eye interest) is balanced throughout the whole so that one sees such work with "vision in motion," a concept of today.

Flower arrangers have been slow in accepting and exploring new possibilities in organizing the elements of design, but the challenge is now gaining momentum among experienced arrangers. This new approach to design offers an important extension to the art of flower arrangement. Instruction is outside the scope of this book but it is important to at least bring attention to the possibility of new assembling techniques.

For those inquisitive about the many aspects of modern arranging, *Modern Art in Flower Arrangement** and *Modern Abstract Flower Arrangements** provide instruction in, and examples of, the most recent developments in flower arrangement. To imply that contemporary modern arranging is superior to traditional is not intended. I mean simply to point out the advisability of an awareness of ever-changing concepts and of technical innovations, so that arrangers can enjoy the products of many variables.

No one style can remain an eternal standard. As an arranger's purpose changes, so does his viewpoint and hence his artistic expression. New insights are open to every far-thinking arranger if he will appreciate and explore the specific direction of *all* art styles and techniques.

*By Emma Hodkinson Cyphers, Hearthside Press, Inc.

80 LEFT MAXIMUM EXPRESSION, MINIMUM MATERIAL *Horse-chestnut bark is se-cured to a board anchored with coal, one piece shaped to fit with a carbon drill. Giant rooted echeveria is braced between the coal chunks with flat wooden dowels.*
ARRANGER: NANCY GAGARIN   PHOTOGRAPHER: JOHN HUGELMEYER

81 RIGHT A DRIED ARRANGEMENT IN TAN AND BROWN *On a walnut base, a bleached redwood burl supports maple columns (legs from an old chair), and leaves of New Zea-land flax looped to enclose space. The resulting shapes are repeated by opuntia distorted by skele-tonizing.*
ARRANGER: MRS. LESTER STANAWAY   PHOTOGRAPHER: L. COVELLO PHOTOS

82　A NEW TREATMENT　　　　Low in the design are leaves and seed capsules of castor-oil plant *Ricinus*. In the higher placements, flesh is carefully removed from the leaves to create unusual pattern with strong vein structures.

ARRANGER: MRS. HOWARD OBERLIN　　　PHOTOGRAPHER: HOWARD OBERLIN

83 FOR A MODERN HOME   A calla lily, curved leaves of sansevieria, and brass rings are compatible with the modern "see-through" vase. The leaves echo the container's color and surface pattern; the base (part of an artist's palette) completes a modern-traditional arrangement.
ARRANGER: MRS. RAYMOND P. WISMER   PHOTOGRAPHER: CLASSIC PHOTO STUDIO

84　FREE AND EASY　On black lacquer planks a blue-green container touched with white carries whitened wire and stems of Asparagus falcatus with its green leaves and darker green foliage.
ARRANGER: FRANCES LOUISE BODE　　PHOTOGRAPHER: WILLIAM T. BODE

85   A MODERN SPACE-FORM   *On a walnut base a handmade ceramic vase—chocolate brown trimmed with golden brown — holds dried honeysuckle branches entwined around a calla leaf and two cut leaf clusters of umbrella-plant in such a way that space is as important as solids in interpreting the subject "Space Age."*

ARRANGER: BERNICE KINNEY   PHOTOGRAPHER: WILLIAM T. BODE

INDEX